DARE TO BUILD IN A BOOM

DARE TO BUILD IN A BOOM

A Love Memoir

TANGEA TANSLEY

Copyright © Tangea Tansley 2023
The moral right of the author has been asserted.

All rights reserved. Without limiting the rights under copyright above, no part of this publication shall be reproduced, stored in or introduced into a retrieval system or transmitted in any form or by any means (electronic, mechanical, photocopying, recording or otherwise), without the prior permission of the copyright owner.

National Library of Australia Cataloguing-in-Publication data
Tansley, Tangea – author.
Dare to Build in a Boom: A love memoir
978-0-9941625-8-8 (paperback)
Tansley, Tangea. Non-fiction. Memoir. History

Cover design: Luke Harris – Working Type Studio
Interior design: Spiro Books
Cover image © Tangea Tansley

For Richard with love

Richard Wheater

Contents

Let's Build a House 1
The Perfect Block 10
In Search of Our Grand Design 25
Plans in Waiting 35
Still Nothing Happens 42
This is Meant to be Fun? 59
Expendable Grandmothers 78
The Darkest Night 112
Then Morning Comes 123
An End in Sight 130
What's In a Name? 143
Later 159

About the Author 165

LET'S BUILD A HOUSE

'You're daft,' said an English friend who had come across from her home in Portugal to stay with us for a spell. 'Sell the house? Why on earth would you want to leave this?' She waved her hand at the view in front of us. 'It has everything you need. It's perfect.'

'It's got the freeway, too,' I'd replied a bit lamely, feeling ungrateful. 'It's intrusive day and night. In the back garden, out here, we can hardly hear ourselves think. And inside, the floor of the family room vibrates.'

'Freeway? What freeway?'

It's true to say that the freeway with its six streams of traffic and a train route scheduled for along the central median strip bothered me more than it did most people. It didn't, for example, worry my husband Richard or the majority of those who came to the many parties we held in that house in Lockhart Street, south of the Swan River. In fact, I don't think they even noticed it. And, to be honest, it hadn't presented a problem the day we bought the property. But it wasn't long before the traffic began to get to me and it wasn't that I didn't try to reason with myself.

Having survived six years in a flat in the heart of Hong Kong alongside the raucous clamour of the day/night fish market, with an enthusiastic panel beater across the road, horse races on radios turned up high every Saturday afternoon and Chinese opera in the evenings, I told myself I could get used to anything. I knew that even though you're convinced you'll go mad that first weekend, a week or two later it's not so bad after all. I know that, in the end, it doesn't become so much a case of blocking it out as genuinely not noticing it.

But, for some reason, it hadn't happened this time. Perhaps it was the contrasting and uncomfortable juxtaposition of the freeway's rowdy rows of flying steel with our pretty garden with its landscaped levels, the bright heads of the standard roses staring back at themselves from the quiet blue of the pool, the avenues of hibiscus and poinsettia. Or maybe it was because I was older than I was in the Hong Kong days and a little less tolerant than I used to be. I don't know. I found myself getting grumpy when we worked in the back garden simply because it was impossible to hear each other speak when a road train rumbled past. Ambulance and fire engine sirens were a regular occurrence. The air brakes of the big trucks, the screeching tires of beat-up cars as the hoons played wheelies and the intermittent blasts of horns punctuated the constant drone of traffic. Too often, in the middle of the night when there were fewer vehicles on the roads, the motorcycle gangs and police car chases took over. Grey dust filtered over the rose bushes. And lead in petrol hadn't yet been banned. Besides, situated as it was between the house and the view of the river, the freeway's eternal whizzing steel made me dizzy.

It was not until we'd been in the house for a couple of years that I tried to discuss it with Richard.

'Doesn't it worry you?' I prompted finally when he didn't reply.

'Well, no. Evidently not half as much as it does you. No, I can't really say it does. I think perhaps you might be exaggerating it somewhat, don't you?'

I envy my husband his attitude, his ability to shrug off the relatively insignificant as unimportant. Along with a pretty young wife and my sister Toni's homeopathic skills, that's how Dad got to live healthily to the brink of his hundredth birthday: by using this knack of not stressing the inconsequential. Or at least what was, in his opinion, inconsequential. 'Let it go, darling,' my father would say, sitting back in his leather wing chair in the little cottage, shaking his fingers as if he were flicking off drips. 'It's not worth worrying about. Just let it go.' So maybe I *was* exaggerating. But that's how it gathered in the corners of my mind: those ribbons of traffic curling around the beauty of that garden.

In the way of women, I had been contemplating change for a while, but I think the exact moment it fixed our lives for the next five or six years was late one lazy summer afternoon as we were having a cup of tea in the shade of the pergola. I set down my cup.

'Richard?'

'Mmm?' He looked up, a slight crease between his eyebrows, his finger firmly anchored on the newspaper article he was reading.

'Let's build a house, darling.'

'A house. What for? We've got a lovely house.' His frown deepened for a moment and then disappeared altogether. 'Build, you say? Build.' He turned the word over in his mind. 'Well, I suppose we can certainly think about it.'

He returned to his reading for all of ten seconds before he reached for the pen in his top pocket and, using the white space around the adverts in the paper, started sketching.

It was as simple as that, the moment things changed.

At least, that appeared to be the moment, but, looking back, I wonder whether it wasn't some time before. Was the freeway the only trigger?

At this point, Richard and I had only been together for a few years. We had both been married before, but in terms of our own relationship, marriage was new. This house we'd bought two years before was our first home together and it was, as I've said, set in an established garden. We both loved gardening and this was the first time either of us had inherited quite such a well-thought-out garden, carefully crafted into a number of levels and inhabited by a raft of different bird species including an owl that nested at the top of one of the two Sultan palms.

The house itself was built in the Sixties and had had only two owners before us which I'm sure contributed to that loved look some properties are lucky enough to portray. Or with houses, too, is attracting the right people something more than luck or chance?

As it happens, we're both handy types, Richard through a natural affinity and I, I suspect, because I'd no choice. Most of my fix-it skills were gained between marriages when I purchased a nineteenth-century weatherboard cottage – simply because it happened to be the cheapest house for sale in the Perth metropolitan area at that time – and proceeded over the next few years to make it livable.

Lockhart Street was quite different. It needed some painting and updating – and, yes, there was a lot of peeling wallpaper to be removed there, too – but overall what had been added over the years had been done thoroughly and with a degree of sensitivity.

We had put our own stamp on the place by getting married in the front garden in an extraordinarily beautiful ceremony presided over by a minister who had been granted special dispensation to hold the ceremony off sanctified territory. He was Michael Rowden, at that time the minister for the chapel at Rottnest, a much-loved island retreat just off the coast of Western Australia. I don't think of myself as a church person, but I'd travel a lot further than Rottnest to attend one of Michael's services. His sermons were real and engaging. He talked about the difficult stuff we face every day, like grief and jealousy and impatience. His congregation didn't just sit and listen, but gathered about him, an integral part of the service, so when you stepped out of the chapel at the end of it all, the power that sits so thickly in every place of worship I've ever visited had become part of you: you stood straighter, feeling somehow more substantial and better able to cope than before. We lacked the necessary connection to Rottnest Island to get married in that lovely chapel, but next best was to be married by Michael in our own garden. Quite aside from that, the house had been the setting for several Christmas parties and both our daughters' engagement parties. And the much-loved Ridgebacks who had passed on in their thirteenth year were buried beside the lemon tree in the back garden.

Lockhart Street had memories and it was ours. It was ours, split equally between us in terms of financial input, and we didn't even owe the bank. It had a picture window view across the freeway to the river from the family room and, facing west, we were privy to some outstanding sunsets which went a long way towards compensating for the glaring summer heat. It had a large lounge and separate dining room, three bedrooms, two bathrooms and a huge dressing room. It had a smart kitchen with jarrah cupboards and plenty of them. It was ours and we were lucky to have it. So what is it about humans that we find ourselves compelled to change things that are working perfectly well? 'If it ain't broke, don't fix it.' A useful piece of advice that has stood me in good stead over the years, but on this occasion I was going to override it.

The traffic was one thing that sooner or later was going to cause us to move, but there was another strong urge that came into play. It could just as easily have been acquisitiveness, but in this case it wasn't. I think it was something more basic. More primal. Something like even though you're getting married later in life than usual or you're mate number two or three or four, you still have that urge to get it together in a more knitted sort of way. Like threading dry grasses together to make a comfy nest. Or procreating. Most newly marrieds go ahead and have kids. But Richard was my third husband and I his second wife. We already had a house and dogs and there was no question of adding to our lovely families – Richard's sons Murray and Mal, his daughter Mhairi, my daughter Tammy and my son Viv – the five children who were at that point young adults marrying and having their own families.

But it was time to face the fact there was an ancient urge stirring in me that until now had been subliminal. And that it wasn't only the pesky freeway that brought the thought of building out into the open that day we sat under the pergola having tea.

There was a further stimulus, too, that was quite separate from, and opposite to, the emotive. Retirement in one form or another was looming in the next five to ten years and, central to potential changes in lifestyle and income, was the fast-fading chance to build a house to suit our own distinct personalities. Miss the next few years and we would not only have missed the opportunity to create something together, but also the chance to live in a home custom-built to suit ourselves. In this way, the house became part of a five-year plan designed to move us from where we were to where we wanted to be.

One weekend, we blocked out the view of the freeway by sticking large sheets of white paper over the width of the family room picture window. First up was to brainstorm our aims and objectives, writing them out large in thick blue Texta ink and giving each dot-point a time frame.

Since by now we'd been together long enough to accumulate what therapists call *issues*, on the next sheet we wrote down our grumbles. In short, we turned our life into columns of pluses and minuses before coming up with what we hoped were solutions to the less than satisfactory. Our analysis ran into the next weekend. And the next. During the working week, we were quite normal ordinary people. But for those three weekends, we were focussed, intense, committed. No strategist could have been more thorough in digging for the essentials and whittling out the dross, no psychologist more searching in the quest for 'truth', no government more artistic with the finances. And then, typically – given the combination of Pisces and Virgo – having worked out what we wanted, we lost no time in starting to turn the dream into reality.

Interestingly, the *issues* were the easiest to sort and it was only later we realised the serendipity in the timeliness of including what was, I suppose, a sort of self-therapy session in our five-year plan. What was going to be a lot harder in the short term, despite our financial juggling, was to find a block at a price that would leave enough over to build something we actually wanted to live in.

Both of us had lived in proximity to both river and city for the past decade or so. We were both working and reluctant to increase both our commuting time and the distance from our families by moving further out. This was, for us, the ideal zone in which build. But it took very few Sunday sorties up, down and around the Canning and Swan rivers to find there was nothing at all – even given the most optimistic purchase – in our price bracket. We'd get more than we paid for the property we were living in, but nothing near what we'd need to buy a block and build in a similar area without the freeway disadvantage.

To create further funds, one thought was to subdivide our present quarter-acre and sell off the bottom half. The block would divide neatly into two with the house in the top portion. With the funds from the lower half, we could purchase a block and live in the house while we built. The proposal fulfilled all Council and subdivision requirements and would provide the funds we needed…and ruin the property in the process. We paced it out, thought it through, and finally decided the property didn't deserve that. Given its surroundings, its oasis of calm was tight enough already and to destroy the lovely garden would be pure greed. It wouldn't have looked good on our final CVs at the pearly gates.

Another possible solution – although time-costly – was along with looking for the perfect property to either renovate or build, we could work on increasing our budget by building a property portfolio. Interest rates were at a 30-year low and it was a buyers' market. What about mortgaging the house and using the collateral to buy an investment property? It started us thinking and, as the mind gurus tell us, the first step towards any solution is for one's mind to become open to possibilities. Not long afterwards, a property investment seminar moved the *possible* one step further. We bought the book *Rich Dad, Poor Dad* and became further convinced. A meeting with our bank relationship manager proved they were only too happy to lend against the house. The only glitch at that stage was the bank's arrogant demand I change my surname on the loan application to that of my husband's…and this in the twenty-first century despite the fact that all my existing bank accounts, passport and other official documents had been in my own name for years. When I politely refused, somewhat to my surprise, I heard nothing further.

Two weeks later we bought our first investment property. I'd come across the *For Sale* sign on a quick diversion one day. Richard did a drive-past in his lunch-hour and we put in an offer that evening for three-quarters of an acre of river land in Cannington fronting onto the Canning

River and ideal for subdivision. Shortly afterwards we bought an office property in a city suburb, the following year, a sub-divisible property in Beckenham just a little further out from the city.

This not only took us to the limit of our borrowing capacity, but also proved to be extremely time-consuming…something they don't emphasise (enough) in property seminars. Richard was working fulltime in the controversial area of biotechnology at the Department of Agriculture. I was working on my PhD thesis, lecturing part-time at university, tutoring at different schools and private houses in the afternoons and ghosting the second half of her biography for Ethnée Holmes à Court which involved spending a day a week at Heytesbury, a horse stud an hour's drive south of Perth. And then actually writing the book in between everything else.

So we were at our respective limits in more ways than one. But our instincts were right: it was a good time to buy and although we weren't to know it then, ultimately it did enable us to achieve our final goal.

I no longer like the *dream house* cliché I used so readily and often back then because I feel its apparent triteness smothers something deeper, with the real *dream* in it all getting overlooked. We use the dream word so unthinkingly to describe something not quite real, something that Tinker Bell might magic into being in a sweep of stardust. Like wanting a house with a courtyard as its soul-centre where we can sit – just sit and be – on summer nights under a fragrant frangipani tree.

But perhaps it's the very intangibility of a dream house that lends it excitement? Remember how we were encouraged to draw a house in pre-school? More often than not it was square (solid) with a roof like a hat (shelter/safety). Even though, in my case, I grew up in the tropics, in my drawings my house always had a chimney with a plume of curling smoke (warmth), four windows and a door. It usually had a garden path (the world coming to the front door) and a yellow sun shining brightly in one corner (happiness, predictability). Invariably I drew my own family to one side of the building: my stick mother and father almost as tall as the house, then me and my little sister. At our feet were at least two large stick dogs. Often a cat with M ears and a curly tail: although we never owned a cat, somehow a cat looked right. Sometimes I added a tree, grass and flowers. We all did it the same way, didn't we? And why? Was it because it was so much more than just a school exercise? Was it because it represented the safe place we all need and don't always get?

By setting out to build our dream house, what were we doing, Richard and I? Creating something that wasn't just your place or my place, but ours? Trying to duplicate the security of childhood by filling in the outlines of the childhood drawing? Bringing something from a dimension outside the real into being? Maybe, on different levels, all of the above. The problem with a dream is that it's something over which we have no control. It can just as easily turn into a nightmare and that was something we had to find out for ourselves.

THE PERFECT BLOCK

Build, for us, was quite a flexible term when we first started to think about building. It covered a number of variations, from starting from the beginning with earthworks and a concrete slab on an empty block to totally gutting and renovating an existing house. Or buying a transportable to live in while building an extension as time and money became available. We explored every option and did our homework thoroughly in the hope that when an opportunity arose we would be ready. In retrospect, however, through our lack of focus, I think we ended up making things harder for ourselves.

For instance, although it was purchased to form part of our investment portfolio and further out from the city than we wanted to live, it wasn't long before we both started to fall for the setting of the land in Cannington. It really was Aussie picture book: a grassy paddock that led down to a grove of paper-bark trees framing a section of river sometimes bluer than the sky where canoeists paddled among families of ducks. It was pure 'country' with an old and rusting corrugated-iron stable to one side of the site and the neighbour's Shetland pony, Toby, to keep the grass in check. Richard's first sketches were for this land and, given this site, the house couldn't be other than traditionally Australian which meant, for us, wide verandahs on three sides and a corrugated-iron roof. The verandahs would be tiled and cool, and as you entered the house you'd have the view of the river in front of you. I'd always lusted after a water view from the entry and here was an opportunity.

From the start, we were determined to ignore the current four bedroom/two bathroom trend. We were building this for ourselves – more specifically for our retirement (at this point in our plan) – and figured all we needed in addition to the living area and study was a bedroom and two bathrooms. To one side of this house, we'd build another dwelling: a lounge/dining area with kitchenette, a smaller bedroom and one bathroom. Two of our children were overseas at the time and this would give them somewhere to stay during their visits or holidays. Or we could let it. Or we could put a kit home on the block to live in while we built the main house, at which point it would revert to the guest house. Choices.

We went to the block each weekend, sometimes just to sit and picnic by the river, other times to help Toby along by slashing at the grass. We also, rather naively, took on the challenge of hacking at the jungle of waterweeds proliferating along the bank which threatened to become almost as great a threat to our stretch of river as the water hyacinth had proved to be to the river systems in Africa. A month later, the plants were back, thicker than ever.

I don't quite know when our plans for the Cannington land changed but – over a period of a couple of years – they did, and sometime later we decided to revert to Plan A, which meant subdividing the land and selling the blocks instead of building.

Meanwhile we continued to rake through the Houses for Sale columns in the daily newspaper and we couldn't pass a Home Open without dropping in. Eventually we came across a house for sale on the river at Brentwood about ten minutes' drive from our current house. The home was architect-designed, the agent told us, and again it had absolute river frontage. You literally walked out through the sliding doors of the main room into the back garden where only a low fence and gate separated the house from this stretch of the river which was, according to the sales spiel, a favourite spot for dolphins. The house had been leased for some years, but didn't have that exhausted look that long-term rental properties sometimes exude. And, yes, it did have the entry door opposite the water, but for some reason out of sync with the view. It had one huge room which would be perfect for our living needs, and five bedrooms, which were not. But it did, as the real estate ads put it, have heaps of potential.

The roof could be extended to cover a verandah which ran alongside the river, and a couple of walls between the smaller bedrooms knocked down to make three large ones.

These were the more obvious changes; there were others, too. Although it was designed by one of Perth's more prominent architects, we were mystified as to why anyone would design a house on a block like this without taking full advantage of the outlook. Having said that, the house *had* something. The attraction wasn't only its riverside location, and changes could be made without doing anything too major in a structural sense.

There was only one snag: its price. A price tag of $1,000,000 that stopped us more effectively than a double-brick wall. This was pre-boom Perth – around 2002 – when the market was chugging along happily enough. The housing explosion in the Eastern States with the red-hot auctions and long queues for rental properties was something one read about in the daily paper and as remote from our lives as news of octuplets born in Dakota. For a rather ordinary house in a still-ordinary suburb that needed a fair amount of money spent on it to make it work, a price tag of that magnitude was something that belonged to the future. But we wanted that house. A lot.

However, as we all know, it's possible to want something a lot and not get it. No matter how often we added together what we might get for Lockhart Street and what we might have made (on paper) since we bought the land in Cannington, we came up with a fairly hefty shortfall. We had about half of what we needed and that was before renovation.

We continued to look in and around the river suburbs. The river has its moods and openness and the view is constantly changing. I love the smell of the sea, but the river is gentler somehow: it lacks the ferocity of the wind, the sand-laden air and restrictive gardening conditions of properties close to the beaches on our West coast. Our search went on for a long time. In all we made four or five somewhat guarded offers: mainly on houses simply because so few empty blocks fell within our financial reach. Were these serious offers? I think so. Certainly they were on the low side compared to the asking price, but that was because the properties would all need a considerable expenditure of time and money to fulfil our particular need.

More than two years had passed since our brainstorming weekend. I had a publisher for the Heytesbury Stud book, and my PhD thesis "Writing from the Shadowlands" on the legacy of the great Edward Said was beginning to take shape. The freeway still bothered me, but the house had a good feel about it and we were happy. At the same time, the market was still in our favour and we knew that when we found the right block or house, we would move on.

In the way of the universe, it was at this relaxed point we found what we had been looking for, although it took us a little while to realise this. While we had trawled the river locations back and forth looking for likely property, we'd missed a little-known suburb that clings to the point that juts out into the Canning River.

My introduction to Salter Point was a spontaneous nature walk along the riverside led by one of Richard's environmental colleagues from the Department of Agriculture. It was a beautiful fresh summery morning with pelicans fishing in a river so still that the reflections of the houses on the far bank stretched upside-down in the water. The paths we followed were sensitively laid out, designed to keep people away from the fragile vegetation while keeping everything as unspoiled and natural as possible. Bright white heron with yellow beaks stood proudly in an inlet; waterfowl – rather like long-legged chooks with ducks' feet and cheeky-looking tails – dived into the bushes as we passed. There were black swans with cygnets in tow, a pod of dolphins playing tag in the water. Impossible to imagine a place as far from the buzz of the freeway as this, and yet only eight minutes from the centre of the city. It was not difficult to fall in love.

After that, we drove the few minutes to Salter Point each weekend, parked the car and walked the dogs along the foreshore, through the paper-bark groves and up the nature trails that clung to the side of the cliff towards the boys' college of Aquinas. Somehow we both knew this was where we'd buy or build, whichever came first. Our weekend walks were supplemented by a drive through our favourite streets whenever we had time. On one of our walks, we did what the real-estate agents do: a letter-box drop in the hope of a likely house coming onto the market. Or, if a property looked ripe for subdivision, we took a deep breath, knocked on the door and asked the owners, politely, whether they were thinking of selling. In all cases, they weren't.

It was on a Sunday we came across a brand new For Sale sign on the subdivision of a property that ran from a pretty laneway called Riverway down to Salter Point Parade alongside the river. The front block was the more expensive of the two and a great deal more attractive than the rear, but further research showed a caveat on the title would restrict the roof height which would mean either a flat roof and/or lower ceilings on our proposed building than we'd like. And although it had stunning and absolute 180-degree river views, its position right on the street enabled the view at the expense of privacy.

Initially, the rear block on its rather intimidating slope up a cliff side – a fall of nine metres from top to bottom – didn't appeal at all. Neither of us was keen on battleaxe blocks with the inherent parking problems. And once the house in front was built, whether the rear house would have any sort of view, other than a possible window of opportunity down the driveway, was doubtful. In fact, the sale sign didn't even use the word *potential* in relation to the view. Instead it hedged with "possible river views from second storey". In addition, this block, too, had a height restriction on the build. Surveyors could make a good guess as to how much of a view we'd end up with, but until the front house was built, it was impossible to guarantee any more than a glimpse. A real no-no with very little going for it, we said to each other. And we weren't alone in our thinking: the front block sold quickly, but the other sat on the market for so long the For Sale sign fell over.

'No one's willing to take it on,' I observed as we strolled past a year or more later. 'But it's been there for such an age the owner might just be desperate to sell.' I looked at Richard. 'Why don't we do something incredibly wild and a bit stupid and make an offer?'

'On that?' He stopped, gazed up at the steep, sandy, lopsided bank with its mass of lantana bushes gone feral. 'Nuts. Cost a fortune in retaining for a start.'

'But we could use that as a bargaining tool, couldn't we?' Sparked by his reticence I warmed rapidly to the idea. 'Why not? We can take that into consideration when we make our offer. Make a cheeky offer? It's been a year, Rich, already a year since we first saw the sign.'

The property was owned by a doctor and his wife and we made an offer that night. Given the length of time it had been on the market and the extensive retaining walls that would have to be erected, we thought we'd try a $370,000 offer on the $450,000 asking price. More than fifteen per cent lower…so low, in fact, we heard nothing back. Not even a counter-bid. It obviously wasn't meant to be. There were other blocks, we consoled ourselves, and continued our search.

Some months passed. We sensed the market was on the turn. There were fewer and fewer properties for sale. Nothing that tempted within our budget. But, meanwhile, each weekend we continued to walk past the difficult block sitting up there on the hillside and one day, despite ourselves, we made a second offer. And then, when those two came to nothing, a third.

The new agent called back a day later. 'The owner's been away,' she said. 'Perhaps that's why you didn't hear. But if you really want it, you'll have to go a lot higher than that…'

It was tempting not to bother, but by now I suspect we wanted the block for an additional set of reasons. The more primitive side of our natures had taken over: we were like kittens chasing a fidgety ball of string, like sharks circling a tuna boat, like a kid who wants a toy either because no-one else has it or someone else has it. It was something we couldn't have – and couldn't really, by this time, afford – with the result that we wanted it even more. Still, we cautioned ourselves, fifteen months had passed and, evidently, we were still the only suckers on the block. So our final, *final* offer was $430,000. This time, the owners countered at $440,000. Exhausted, we signed the deal.

There was one small, but useful, financial upside to this: the title wasn't immediately available, which meant we didn't have to start repayments for a while. Fortunately. The first of many lessons came at this point, too. Although we had been frustrated and somewhat miffed that the doctor had not countered our first two offers, in retrospect his negotiation skills were admirable. He had set what he believed to be a fair price: if we wanted the property, we could pay the price. Or pass it by.

For some time we'd been in the process of subdividing the Cannington land into three separate blocks. We needed the sale of those blocks to finance our purchase and there didn't appear to be any way of speeding things up. Because the Western Australian Planning Commission (WAPC) issues a job number, you can simply log in to see where you are in the queue without disturbing a real person. (Remember, this was in the early days of the de-humanised online world.) Great. But the system breaks down when the time period set by the Commission itself for the subdivision determination has elapsed by some months, when there's no information other than 'pending' on the electronic file and when no one in the organization can track down a paper version.

Eventually I was put on to a charming and efficient-sounding officer who promised he would look into it and get back to me. A day later, true to his word, he did.

'The problem with your application is that it comprises what we call river land which takes somewhat longer to process. You are, after all, professional developers.'

'Professional developers? No, not at all. I mean, we're hoping to subdivide this portion of land, but we're certainly not professionals. We're brand new at all this.'

'Hmm…' He sounded doubtful. 'Well, anyway, the reason for the delay is that your land borders the river. And when you subdivide river-land, half of it returns to the government…'

'Half of it? That's…*half* the three-quarter-acre? Do you mean that the government just…well…takes it?' I felt sick.

'We pay you for it. Fair market value. It's a question of negotiation.'

'I see.'

'There's also a proportion of the remaining portion of land that will have to be returned to local council: in your case, for a bicycle path between your land and what will be government land. So we'll require you to re-submit your application accordingly. In other words, each lot will be something less than one-eighth of an acre instead of the current quarter-acre.'

'I see.'

'That's what's taking the time. And there's something else. That area of Cannington may be subject to aircraft noise. We're just working on this actually…and we might insist on a memorial to that effect being placed on the title.'

'But we're down there quite often and the planes aren't any more intrusive than anywhere else,' I protested. 'In fact, it's an incredibly peaceful spot. And I wonder why all this didn't appear on the title when we bought the land two years ago?'

'We're currently looking into all this. It's not yet finalized. I'm just warning you. As a courtesy.'

'Thank you.' I hung up and stood for a while leaning against the kitchen counter: with less than half the land available, would we even get our money back?

A day or so later, another phone call from the officer, his voice light and enthused, sounding as if he'd just won Lotto.

'You'll never guess what else I've uncovered.'

'What?' Perhaps there would be no memorial about noisy planes? Perhaps he had some news about the value of the river land? My heart skipped. 'Good news?'

'Well, that depends on how you look at it, but I must say I'm surprised no one's dug it up before now. That land of yours, did you know it was subject to the 100-year flood rule?'

'100-year flood?' This was some years before changing climatic conditions would force us into greater awareness and I wasn't exactly sure what he meant.

'What I'm saying is that your property falls within the flood zone which means that the building line will have to be so far back from the river I don't think there'll be much room for dwellings on your blocks. Let me see… Yes, the flood-line runs on an angle right through the property. On the diagonal. We'll be sending you details of this along with the conditions, but I thought you'd like to know.'

'How much is left?'

'Not a lot.'

'Do you know what the approximate building area might be?'

'As I said, there won't be a lot left to play with, but I won't know exactly until I've had it drawn up.'

'But there was no flood-line shown on the title when we bought the property.'

'Well, there should have been. As I say, it's something I've just uncovered. Seems like you've bought a dog, doesn't it? Have a good day,' he said cheerfully and rung off.

It's easy to be wise in retrospect, but in looking back, with climate change now a harsh reality, we can only be heartily glad the officer picked up on the flood zoning when he did. And, as it turned out, we didn't do too badly out of the Cannington subdivision. Several years later we sold the third and final block for well over what we'd paid for the original property. But that was due to the market turning in our favour and not before we'd spent a small fortune on surveyors, valuers, earthworks, extensive and expensive retaining walls and received a fraction of what had been independently assessed as 'fair market value' for half the land from the State Government. I'm not sure whether all this comes under the heading of *caveat emptor* or experience. I know only that my twin qualities of optimism and enthusiasm have combined throughout my life to carry me into some interesting situations most of which, fortunately, have turned out positively over time.

What's the alternative, I wonder? Sitting on a river bank watching opportunities sail by? I'd rather play Monopoly than snakes and ladders any day, but quite apart from the experience gained, it's a rare mistake that doesn't have an upside. Or another quote: 'If you can't stand the heat in the kitchen, you shouldn't be there'. We like to cook and that takes heat. So be it.

On the other hand, we don't deliberately expose ourselves to boiling oil or naked flame, so during the lengthy process of our Salter Point purchase in an endeavour to avoid the sort of unpleasant surprises we'd stumbled into with the Cannington property, we checked Council by-laws, familiarized ourselves with the R-Codes, and found out what we required in terms of the width of the driveway, any and all setbacks, overlooking laws and general prohibitions in the hope that once we started designing, the process would be as quick and efficient as possible.

The block wasn't a perfect fit. We knew we'd taken on a chunk of land that would require a great deal of retaining. Not only would this be expensive, but in order to take advantage of the "possible view" the building would have to be more than one storey and that, too, would be more expensive. On our evening visits to the block we struggled up the sandy slope to squint along a stick pointed at the opposite river bank, but there was no real way to tell how much of the river we'd be able to see. There were other negatives, too, like the battleaxe block with the accompanying inconveniences of restrictive parking and turning circles. And the neighbouring dwellings. The house on the southern boundary comprised several stories of dark brown brick, an unbroken wall of which faced our land and towered darkly above everything else in the vicinity.

The other thing we had to do – and in the end we did with mixed feelings – was to put the Lockhart Street house on the market. Although we'd started talking to builders who estimated our new house would take around five or six months to build, there was no knowing how long the current house might take to sell and we figured the safest thing to do was to move into a rental for the duration of the project.

Shortly after we put the house up for sale, a woman knocked on the door. Her family had emigrated from England several decades before, she said, and her father had built the house based on a design their mother had saved from an English *Homes & Garden* magazine.

For years, the daughter had walked past the house on her way to work, but until she saw the For Sale sign she'd lacked the courage to introduce herself. The two sisters came for drinks one evening and we sat on the verandah with one of their photograph albums, all of us captivated by the photos of the house as it had been in their childhood. Was it the youth of the children in the photographs that gave the house its look of wide-eyed innocence? Or do houses, too, lose their innocence as they age? Whatever it was, the house in its early pictures looked so young and, yes, naïve.

Later we all wandered around both house and garden while they explained some of the idiosyncrasies we hadn't been able to work out: like why the staircase in the hallway faced the wrong way (a space problem) and why a thick jarrah post was set in the centre of one of the upstairs bedrooms (to hold up the roof). They rediscovered where they had built their first cubby, remembered the dogs they'd had and the ease back then of strolling to the river without a six-lane highway as a barrier. They pointed out where they'd helped their dad with the painting and recalled the look on their father's face at their mother's insistence a particular design of wallpaper be imported from England. Thirty years fell away and they were kids again. Their old home curled around them. You only had to watch those sisters relate to each other and to their old home to know without a doubt a house has a spirit.

That's why I prefer not to return to a property once I've sold or moved on. And the more I've connected with the place in terms of length of stay or physical and imaginative input, there's a bond that's difficult to describe and I'd rather take a longer route than drive past.

But there were a couple of exceptions: one being my first house, a 1940s dwelling that had been rented for ten years or more before I bought it back in the 1980s. When I moved in, it was in a shocking state with sagging doors and broken windows, locks missing, holes in the plaster and the only kitchen cupboard a soggy, swollen chipboard mess. Almost worst of all, in the fashion of its era, the toilet was outside, down the back steps from the kitchen. Daytime was all right, but at night it was downright scary. The poisonous Redback spiders and their assorted friends had made it theirs for years and continued to return as quickly as they were swept out. But it wasn't the spiders I was scared of most. It was the unknown people who had broken the windows and kicked in the doors. Many a night I sat on that toilet with a torch in one hand and an old Masai spear in the other waiting for the darkness in front of me to move.

For years after I sold it, I'd driven within a minute of the house dozens of times, but could never bring myself to visit. And then one day, I thought, well, no harm in ducking off the highway and driving by. But the only problem with driving by is that it doesn't stop there. You know the situation that arises in dreams where you are standing back watching yourself? That sense of not being you, but of being an observer in your own life? Well, that was what happened then. Watching myself get out of the car. Seeing the ship's lantern my father had bought for me in Hong Kong still hanging by the front door. Remembering the passage door with its dicey lock that Dad said only needed a shot of oil to make it work. He'd handed me a plastic oil bottle.

'I'll move the handle up and down while you squeeze in the oil. Wait a second while I go around the other side of the door,' he said. 'Okay. Now. Shoot.'

I'd squeezed firmly. There was a yell from the other side and a furious father appeared from around the door, tearing off his spectacles. I protested that I hadn't known he was going to put his eye to the keyhole. It was just as well he'd been wearing glasses. As it was, the damage was fortunately restricted to a dribble of oil down his red tie.

'Thekla will kill me,' he moaned. And then, still cross: 'The idea is to trickle the oil into the lock, not shoot it through the other side.' Gingerly we dabbed the tie with washing-up liquid, so by the time Thekla arrived it was nearly dry and you'd have had to know it was there to see it. It must have been all right, because shortly afterwards she agreed to be his wife and they were married until his death twenty-five years later.

Memories pressed in on me from all sides as I wandered down the adjacent laneway and looked over the back gate into the rear garden, stumbling a bit, mumbling, and wishing I'd brought the box of tissues from the car. I looked back up at the house to find it almost unchanged. But places you've loved don't stop at noting the changes that have taken place. They pull you back into the past you shared. So there were the Ridgeback brothers as puppies chewing their way through the reticulation and then as adult dogs who should have known better, dragging packets of flour, custard and sugar – in fact, anything that came packed in a cardboard box – off the open pantry shelves to make a cake in the middle of the dining room floor. And the parties with friends long moved on, but you could still see the setting sun glinting off the bubbles in the champagne cocktails, still hear the laughter, remember the jokes. And there was the time I played Mrs Memory after the death of my second husband. The house was up for sale and I was sweeping the back steps when a young couple came to look over it. They didn't know I was the owner and I didn't tell them but answered all their questions and was left feeling then and for years after as if I've lived many lives in the one I have now.

But now we had our Lockhart Street house on the market and were looking for a suitable rental. It was at this point an old friend called.

'Hello…hello…long time no hear. Did you know you've bought the block that belongs to one of my near neighbours? I'm giving a party so current residents can meet newcomers. Bring a plate. Seven o'clock. Saturday week.'

By the time we arrived about 100 or so people were gathered on a broad sweep of lawn overlooking the river and it wasn't long before we started chatting. It turned out that Jane and her husband were also in the middle of building a new house in the next street up from our new block.

'And what about you,' she asked. 'Are you long-term residents or new?'

'We've only just bought. A block.' Richard said. 'We don't even have title yet.'

'But we had our first meeting with Council yesterday,' I added.

'Council?' she said, rocking back and forth on her heels. 'Oh, don't mention Council to Robert. Rob, Rob… he's gone to find us a drink. Oh there you are. This is Tangea and Richard…and they're about to build… You have to tell them, Robert. Tell them what they're in for.' She turned back to us. 'Really,' she said, 'you know that park just along the road with the lovely gum trees? Well, it saved our life, that park. We used to take a picnic there and after we'd finished our bottle of red, we could just about cope again. It was like that…' From Council to builder and back again, their tales took us through more than one bottle of champagne and two hours later we parted good friends.

'Tim Tams,' she yelled after us. 'Somebody said a packet of chocolate Tim Tams smoothes the passage through Council. Give it a go, why don't you!'

That night we arrived home still laughing. How difficult is it, after all, to build a house?

IN SEARCH OF OUR GRAND DESIGN

The design Richard had sketched for Cannington won't work for the Salter Point block. For a start, the exaggerated slope of the new site lends itself to an undercroft garage or undercroft something: even if it's just an area for the two little rescue Chihuahuas to lie in the cool as they might in a home on stilts designed for the tropics.

'Perhaps,' I suggest uneasily, 'we'd better stick to what we can afford first up. With a view to adding on later?' The obvious negative to this is that a battleaxe block with half a house built, a garden already in place, and established houses to each side as well as fore and aft, isn't going to lend itself to extensive later-date site works.

We're in a sort of Catch 22. Until we have a plan we can't get a realistic quote, but without knowing what we can get for our budget it's difficult to know where to start.

Meanwhile, the Lockhart Street house eventually sells and in February 2003 we move into an almost-new townhouse. Its pluses lie in its convenience: it's only about ten minutes from the new build and a few minutes from Richard's office, which means he's able to come home for lunch. And it's secure for the dogs with sufficient lawn area out back. Richard is still working fulltime and I'm busy checking the proofs of the Heytesbury Stud memoir. I'm also lecturing part-time at Notre Dame University, finalising my thesis at Murdoch University with a paper to give at a Humanities conference in Greece in July as well as managing the rental properties we still own. In between, I'm working on the draft of my first novel. But it's still sad to let go of our lovely garden. I try not to think of this, cancel it out with the reality we'll both be so busy over the next year there'll be little time to spare anyway. Certainly no time to maintain a large garden. The rental is adequate.

Richard is about to sign the lease, his hand hovering over the contract, when he stops. He looks up at me.

'Six months? Or nine?'

'Six is tempting. But perhaps we should say nine. Just to be on the safe side.' So nine months it is.

When Richard sits down to draw up a plan of the interior of our new house, his ideas flow onto the paper as if they've been ripening in his mind for some time. In the beginning, it's quite simple.

Because it worked so well for us in Lockhart Street, he duplicates the layout of the living room with the study at one end and the kitchen at the other. This main room will have bifold doors along its two long sides to open up completely to the balcony on the river side and onto what will one day be a grassed courtyard on the other. Our bedroom – with our own bathroom and dressing room on either side – will form a wing of its own, set at right angles to the living area and thus also opening onto the courtyard.

Since the block is oriented east-west, the L-shape will enable us to take advantage of the northern aspect by letting winter warmth and light into the centre of our southern-hemisphere home. Meanwhile, however, a large two-storey house is currently being built on the empty block to the north, so for the sake of both privacy and aesthetics, it suddenly makes sense to wall off the courtyard on the other side. As a result, what starts as one of the courtyard walls becomes, with Richard's rapid pencil strokes, a second bedroom and guest toilet with a laundry at the far end leading out onto a drying green at the back.

In terms of passive solar, this version of the plan is even better in that we now have the two bedroom wings of the house oriented towards the north with a high garden wall at the back of the block. The undercroft will take care of car parking, storage space and a workshop for Richard. The

IN SEARCH OF OUR GRAND DESIGN

stairs to the first floor will run up the outside of the building just as they do in our rental townhouse. Inconvenient, perhaps, when it rains. But this is Perth in a State more used to drought and water restrictions than rain. We both like this sketch, start looking for a draftsman and accumulating 'home' magazines and books. Before long I find a draftsman happy to take on the job.

Taking our scribbles we go to meet him together, and when I walk in I like him immediately. If our plan takes him aback he doesn't show it. He's shy and unpushy and altogether nice.

To give him some idea of the essence we're after, I've written down some of the key points we're aiming for:

- a building that's not going to broadcast its age, but its soul might stem from the countries that surround the Mediterranean – northern Africa, Spain, Italy, some of the Arab countries
- space and light…lots of large windows, tiled floors and recycled timber
- an elegant house, but one that says warm and friendly and avoids ostentation at all costs
- built to take advantage of potential views – height of the house in front is capped
- a courtyard in the middle that's large enough to contain grass, trees and shrubs; we don't want a hot and stuffy atrium
- as open-plan as practical
- a solar-wise house with as many 'green' options as possible including such things as termite mesh instead of spraying
- our not very flexible budget: from what we see advertised we think around $250,000 will get us the house we're after.

He says he understands exactly what we're trying to achieve, and he will, he says, formalize our drawings over the next week. As we're about to get in the car I give Richard a hug.

'I feel good about him, don't you? He seems to know precisely what we want.' Richard smiles back, but looks a little unconvinced.

The week drags by. But the following Monday, the draftsman calls.

'I've something on paper for you. Plus some elevations I think you'll like.'

It's a hot day and when I arrive he has the air conditioner on. He unrolls the drawings and smoothes the paper flat on the table between us.

The plan in front of me is of a two-storey building, post-war in mood, very square – no, not just very square, but *very very* square – with grey walls and an orange roof. Actually, apart from the depressing battleship grey of the walls, the elevation is not too different from the childhood house drawings I mentioned earlier. Only it's taller, with a narrow stretch of balcony at the front and a hole in the middle like a doughnut. He points all this out to me as I sit, quite dumb, wondering how I'm going to break it to him that this is as opposite as I can imagine to what we're after. He's creative, I tell myself; with creative people you have to be a bit gentle.

But he's speaking.

'Quite frankly, if you want my advice, you're going about this the wrong way. The cheapest house to build is square…' He runs his forefinger around the drawing for emphasis. 'Like this. See? Four walls with a roof.' In case I don't get it, he drags a smaller piece of paper towards him, re-sketches the square in front of me. Four walls with a roof. 'Right?' He jabs at the hole in the centre of the roof where the courtyard was going to live. 'With this sort of approach you're just making trouble for yourselves. To tell you the truth, I had a great deal of difficulty with it myself. Getting the roof elevation to work is the problem…my software just isn't designed to cope with this sort of thing.' He traces his pen slowly around the outside of the building and then around the perimeter inside. 'You're just wasting money here. This hole in the middle of the house, for example, could be another room. And look, look here…' Again, his pen runs around the outside and inside of the building. He must think I'm slow. Come to think of it, I *feel* slow.

'Can't you see here, *two* perimeters? That means, quite apart from the difficulties you'll have with the roofline, *two* sets of outer walls, therefore *two* sets of double brick. More expense. All more expense. Don't you see? And what will you end up with?' I shake my head. He settles back in his chair, tosses his pen onto his desk, laces his fingers. 'Blowing your budget, that's what. Wasting your money.'

The air conditioner takes over in the gap between his words, sounding not unlike an old washing machine I once had that you could hear from a street away. I wish now I hadn't mentioned budget. Yes, it's important, critical in fact, but for us so is getting something that isn't your ordinary straight-up-and-down-two-storey house. This is so far from that edgy balance between east and west I had envisaged that I wonder whether he's got us mixed up with another client.

When later I place the elevation in front of Richard, I feel as let down as I did when I was a kid and stumbled across carefully hidden Easter eggs only to find they were the ones I hated with the canary-yellow filling which was meant to resemble yolk, but tasted even yuckier.

But we don't give up on him straightaway and it takes two further visits before we're forced to concede we don't have a fit. We do have some sort of a floor plan, a drawn-to-scale version of Richard's sketch, but time is moving along and we're already one month into our nine-month lease without a proper set of drawings to show for it.

Another way around this build is to approach the building companies direct. They have their own designers and will know what they can achieve within our budget.

We choose two to start with, one of Perth's more renowned builders with an excellent reputation for finesse and another company that claims to build Balinese-style houses. Again, we don't want the house to be pigeonholed in terms of style, but we're looking for someone brave enough to design and build outside the literal square.

The representative of the larger building company is also the firm's top designer and a delight to work with. But the front elevation he presents is all triangles of floating steel and sheet glass, more like a commercial building and not at all what we had in mind. In his plan of the building, once again he has pretty much duplicated Richard's sketch, except that our bedroom has been moved from its courtyard position to the front of the house.

'Why?' I ask.

'To take advantage of the view.'

'But we're in bed asleep most of the time and we rather like the idea of the bedroom opening onto the privacy of the courtyard. If we have it at the front of the house, we'll have to have the curtains drawn...' In the end it comes down to 'a take-it-or-leave-it' option.

As for the Indonesian builder. Quite apart from the lack of quality in the finish of his show home – chipped tiles, rough plastering and poorly finished wood which he assures us is a deliberate effort on the part of the company to err in the name of authenticity – he refuses to give us a firm quotation until we sign up. Which strikes us as a little odd. And unsatisfactory.

Next we approach the project builders, but when they see the outline of what we're proposing and the difficulties the block itself presents, their enthusiasm evaporates. Budget doesn't even come into it. Two close friends individually recommend builder contacts and in both cases we have initial meetings that sound promising and come to nothing.

At the time, we thought it was just the difficulties of building something different on a challenging block; it wasn't until later we were to realize that, unbeknown to us, the Eastern States' boom had crossed the Nullarbor and was well and truly in our backyard. For once, even the media were slow to pick it up. Auctions have never been particularly successful in the West, but certainly sales were mounting with people queueing overnight for land releases in the south of the State. So, yes, one problem was an unusual design on a tricky block, but that wasn't the whole story. Why go out of your way to take on a complex project when you suspect you've enough work coming through the door to keep you busy for the next three years? But we didn't know it then.

Meanwhile, despite our careful checks before signing, an unexpected problem emerges on the block itself. We get a call from the agent telling us that when we receive the title it will show an easement.

'What sort of easement?'

'For a sewerage pipe that services the property above you and the property below and runs down one side of your block on your northern boundary. It means you can't build on that four-metre-wide strip that runs adjacent to the boundary line from front to back of your property.'

'But we've already gone some way with our house plans. We need every metre across the width of the block. Setbacks aside, the building pretty much runs from one side to the other. Isn't it rather late to inform us of this? Shouldn't it have been shown on the Offer and Acceptance? Does it have to go down that side of the property, which is fragile and difficult anyway? Can't it run alongside the big retaining wall on the other side?'

This shouldn't have happened, but it did. We contact the firm of surveyors involved who admit as much.

'But at the same time,' the principal says, 'we do a lot of work for the vendor. He pays our bills on time and we value the relationship. There's nothing I can do. And no, it can't go down the other side. We don't want to risk undermining that enormous retaining wall.' In the end, after meetings with representatives of the Water Corporation on site, after examining all our options including expensive legal representation and the equally costly route of either piling or encasing the pipe in concrete, we have no choice but to compromise the size and shape of the house. Effectively this means four metres off its width which will have a considerable impact on the size of each room.

'Maybe we *do* need an architect. We have the ideas, but we need someone to make it workable. We need a front elevation that's not like every other two-storey in town. In fact, now I come to think of it, rooms are rooms…and we know pretty much where we want them and what we want from them. More than anything else what we now need to know is what it's going to look like from the front.'

I call up the Housing Industry Association, try to impart just what it is we're trying to achieve and we act on their recommendation.

The architect's office is plusher than the others, the walls hung about with framed certificates and awards, and the architect is just as pleasant and attentive to our needs as the draftsman. He explains his fee structure, which includes managing the build. We say we're happy to oversee the house ourselves through construction, but that our current concern is what it will look like. In other words, what we need more than anything else is the front elevation. We explain about the possible view we need to take into consideration, about the courtyard, about the mood we're trying to achieve. He parades us past models of his recent designs and in the end gives us a book of glossy photos to look through. Admirable though the designs are, I try to find some correlation between what we're trying to describe and what I see in front of me. He can see I'm struggling and he takes the picture book from me, puts it gently back on the shelf.

'Look, this is not my usual project, but I think I can help. Leave your ideas with me and I'll knock them into shape and you can see what you think.'

We meet with him again a week later. He's taken the trouble to visit the block in the meantime and he has an elevation that we think is moving in the right direction although along the way it's gained a sort of Gothic look with narrow, almost slit, windows along the facade. You wouldn't be surprised to see five-and-twenty blackbirds fly from windows like this.

'We were thinking of a larger expanse of window to the riverside. That's our view, you see…'

'View?' He laughs. 'I'm afraid once that house in front goes up, you can forget the view.'

'But there's a height restriction on the house in front.'

'Even so.' He shrugs. 'In my opinion you're too far back from the river to see much. I think all this view stuff is overrated anyway: you'd be much better off to concentrate on getting the inside of the house right. Besides, facing east as it does, you'll find the morning sun a big problem in summer if you go for large windows along the front.'

Perhaps he's right about the view. I have a mental flashback of my father looking out over the lights of Table Mountain from our home in Cape Town when I was a small child. 'Goodnight, fairyland,' he'd say as he drew the curtains. 'After a while we no longer noticed the view,' I remember my mother saying more than once.

But the architect has re-drawn the internal plan and the courtyard looks better in this iteration. At least it has been restored to the dimensions of Richard's original sketch. But my bathroom has been downsized and the downstairs bedroom with its own bathroom has disappeared completely. Why?

'Put something like that in front of Council and you're asking for problems,' he says of the downstairs changes. 'If you want to reinstate it, no real problem, but we'll have to call it something like a gym and activity room on the plans or else they'll get it into their head it's a separate dwelling and your rates will rise accordingly.'

'But it's not a separate dwelling. It's downstairs in the same building.'

'Even so. Take my word for it: it makes them edgy.'

Bearing Jane and Rob's experiences in mind, the last thing we want is an edgy Council. I have mixed feelings as we leave his office and we don't say much to each other as we drive home.

'At least.' I say to Richard later. 'At least now we've got somewhere with the front elevation.'

'We have?' He gives me the look that husbands sometimes give their wives, but shouldn't, goes to the filing cabinet and draws out a copy of the drawing we'd left with the architect. 'Actually I can't see it's very much different from mine, can you? Except the windows are like arrow slits and the pitch of the roof somewhat higher. And the problem here is that if we have the three-metre high internal walls we'd like, and if we want a chance of looking over the house in front, we're stuck with the minimum pitch anyway because of the zoning laws. So this steeper roof doesn't work.' We look at each other glumly. He drops the drawing back in the drawer. 'Back to square one, I'd say.'

PLANS IN WAITING

It's time to get input from Council and start to establish a working relationship. At least we have something on paper that's going in the right direction and before we have plans we're too attached to, it makes sense to uncover any lurking problems with the design so far. So I make an appointment with Front Counter to discuss our project with their top guy.

'Interesting,' he says when he sees the plans. 'It's always nice to see something different.' As you might guess, at this point, with no one else having appreciated what we're trying to achieve, such a compliment possibly goes further than intended. I smile back. We're unlikely to need Tim Tams here. And then he jabs his forefinger at the undercroft. 'What's this? Storerooms? One, two, three. What are you going to use these for?'

It's a nice day out there with a touch of autumn in the air and I feel a little lightheaded, flippant almost, but something tells me that flippancy at Front Counter is a dangerous idea.

'Well, our idea is to use the first as a cellar, the second for gardening bits and pieces like the lawnmower, edger and so forth, and the third is for suitcases and the stuff the kids tend to leave with us from time to time. And this one here…this sort of loft area over the workshop is for storing timber. We'll be doing a lot on this house ourselves.' I smile brightly. 'Actually we're such untidy people my husband reckons we should build a house as one big cupboard…just for us.'

Shelley Berman, the American comedian, used to joke about the sound of one hand clapping, I think he was talking about the complete and absolute powerlessness of the comedian when a joke falls flat. Or the wobbly feel of a smile held too long without reciprocation. Either of which can nip the edge neatly off the spirit. Because now this guy's convinced himself that the stores may be used for nefarious purposes.

'I'd advise you to cut back on them. Too many stores.'

But he likes the gym and the activity room and I offer up thanks through clenched palms. The courtyard, too, doesn't present a problem – to my surprise. I had been waiting for worries about pests, or problems with too much hot or cold. But the wraparound balcony does.

'You can't have this. You'll be overlooking the house next door. So if you keep it, you'll have to block off the end in some way. And I think you might be in for a problem with the house in front of that one, too.' I hold my breath. We've already had to cut four metres off the width; the house is well back on the property anyway, only leaving enough room at the rear of the property for a narrow strip of vegetable garden and a drying green. He drops his ruler on the drawing, measures from the edge of the balcony to the corner of the house diagonally opposite. 'If you reduce the length of the balcony by, say, three or four metres you should be all right. But you'll have to have some sort of screen at the end regardless.'

'But what about the house directly in front of us? Are we all right there? We'll overlook them, too, from the balcony height.'

'Oh, we don't worry about the house in front. It's primarily the neighbours alongside and off to the diagonal that concerns us in terms of overlooking.'

So, that's all. Stores and balcony. Driving home, I know Richard will be disappointed by the reduced storage in particular, but overall I think we've gotten off lightly and I wonder what all the fuss is about.

Along with the search for a builder, we start in on some of the decision-making, the bigger stuff first: limestone retaining walls, doors and windows, pillars and roof tiles. It's this last that proves the most difficult.

The choice between corrugated iron and tile for the roof is an easy one. Where the Cannington design called for a corrugated-iron roof, this one definitely lends itself to tile. But from there it gets more complicated with choices to be made between concrete and clay (given the only-too-relevant cost saving of the first), different profiles, colours, combinations. We spend hours over the displays, collect samples, trawl websites. On a trip to Singapore, I fall in love with the tiles on the buildings of the CHIJMES complex, but we're unable to track down the builder. And then we find tiles we like on a website and pay for samples to be shipped over. Once we receive them, the product still appeals, but when they demand payment in advance, needless to say, the deal doesn't go ahead. I follow all sorts of leads in search of the right tile: tour past the houses that front the Swan River, check out those at the seaside, take note of those in the hills. In the end, we decide our favourite tiles are on two rather lovely houses in the neighbouring suburb of Applecross, both of which provide a lot of the mood we're trying to capture.

One in particular appeals. I'm driving by one day when, on impulse, I decide to knock on the door. I think I'm surprised when it opens, but I'm not surprised by the owner's enquiring smile, nor that the view down the hall is as lovely as the house is from the outside.

'This is rather a cheek, I know, but we've been admiring your roof tiles from afar for quite a while. We're about to build and wonder whether you can remember where you got them?'

Is it serendipity she not only remembers the name of the architect/builder who had imported the tiles, but that he's known to me because his wife and I had become acquainted at university some time back? We had lost touch until two years ago when she had contacted me about writing a book on their experiences of expatriate life in France. The house owner gives us an address and we set about trying to locate Julie and her husband to see if there's a chance he has stocks of the tiles in Western Australia and, if not, whether he can bring more across from the Continent.

But in the meantime we're still searching for the right person to build this house, so it's like a basket of fortune cookies landing in our laps when we become progressively impressed with the quality of the building of two new houses across the road from our townhouse rental.

Our informal chat with a neighbour only confirms what we can see with our own hopeful eyes: that these houses are being erected by a builder who knows his stuff. And when we finally arrange a meeting, we're as impressed with Emmanuel as we are with his work. He's Italian, a small man, all enthusiasm and energy, with a clear straight gaze, and he and Richard get on famously discussing his early days as a pattern-maker in England.

On subsequent meetings, we only like him more. Although by now we have two other builders who seem keen to take on the challenge, we both sense he's the right man for our house.

He gesticulates away my worries about our tight budget…the one thing, the only thing, that bothers him at the start is the inadequacy of the drawings.

'My daughter is an architect over East and I'm trying to tempt her across to Perth. This project here…it's just right for her. I wonder… She should be here in about three months, sometime in August. Would you be prepared to wait?'

'Three months!' I screw up my face. 'Ouch.' My disappointment whistles round the table.

'Yes, yes, I know. But I would strongly recommend you get someone, anyone, to draw up the plans properly. I can't build on what you have here. Impossible. Quite impossible. There's not enough detail. I can't even quote with any accuracy on this. I need working drawings, structural drawings. And some of this design…' He shakes his head. 'You see, this wing here, it's a waste. You have a powder room and one bedroom where you could do this.' He takes a pen out of his pocket and Richard flips a notepad across the table. 'Make it into two bedrooms with a bathroom in between. The bathroom can still be used as a powder room.'

'But that means we have three beds and three bathrooms upstairs and another set downstairs. We're trying to keep this within budget. And we're not looking for a big house. We don't need one. This is our retirement home.'

'But it's not going to cost more. Not really. Not much more really to get a much more valuable house…a more workable building altogether.' He pauses. 'And these stairs. Stairs outside for a house like this?'

'That's what we've got in the townhouse we're renting. And it works fine.'

'But when it rains?'

I shrug. Rain is rain and in Perth it doesn't happen so often anyway. I feel as if I'm being sucked backwards. We really don't want to go back to the start again.

He shakes his head, sketches again. Quickly. 'Instead you could do this. Bring these stairs inside. By doing this, you are creating a much better house.'

Again I demur, but he's not listening.

'The kitchen, too, should be the other end of the main room…more space.' He flings his pencil onto the pad. 'You need more work on this. If you decide you'd like my daughter's input, let me know. I can give you her phone number. You can fax her the drawings and she might even be able to start work on it before she gets here.'

We take the number and tell him we'll think on it. Shortly afterwards he finishes his coffee and leaves. As he goes out I hear him say, not exactly to me, but not quite under his breath either, 'I hope I get this job.'

'It might be worth waiting for the daughter,' says Richard later.

I'm doing the washing up at the time and his words turn the sudsy water flat.

'Three months?' I groan.

'Tange. It's the end of May already. You're leaving for Cambridge in a week. You'll be away until mid-July…'

'I was hoping that we could sign up with someone before I went away. We've stuffed around for too long already.'

'I think we should wait. We both like him and think he can do the job. And as he said, we can fax the drawings to his daughter, explain what we have in mind, and she can be working on it meanwhile.'

In the mail that night we receive notification that the titles are in order for dealing at Salter Point. That means twenty-eight days to settlement. Twenty-eight days until we have to start paying for the block.

Emmanuel's daughter sounds lovely on the phone. Warm and efficient and we like the idea of a father/daughter team working on the house. We explain to her what we're trying to achieve with this build and she understands perfectly. We arrange to fax our plans and she'll quote for re-drawing them to her father's specifications. Too easy!

It's in this forced interregnum that we make changes. Suddenly it makes sense to have a formal dining room along the fourth aspect of the courtyard instead of a wall. Because of the bifold doors either side of the main room, there is very little actual wall space in this house for our prints and paintings, but if we had one long room that we could also use for dining… *Voilà*! The best of all worlds. Since we need to have the plans redrawn anyway, we might as well include this.

'It'll be narrowish because of the space, but there's plenty of room for a dining table and we could call it a gallery?' I say to Richard.

'Yes, and have another set of bifolds leading from that room out to the courtyard? How about that? Great for parties: we can open up the house from front to back with the grassed area in the middle.' And with that the house gains yet another room.

'It's growing,' I say. 'A bit like a trip through Wonderland.' An insight that will prove to be eerily spot on.

It's during this time, too, that we come across the concept of 'lock-up'. Not lock up in terms of a prison, but building a house to lock-up stage where the builder builds the main structure, including walls, roof, windows, outside doors and possibly ceilings, so that the house can literally be locked up. And thus secure. We were to find out that the reality is that it's "secure" to the point where you have shelter. Basic shelter. What you really have is a shell.

Richard has found an article that cites the pluses and minuses of building this way. He passes the magazine across to me. "Not for everyone," we read. "But an option that enables you to have more control over the finishing of your house as well as enabling you to complete it in your own time as funds become available."

Lock-up. We turn the concept over in our minds. This house has grown so much on paper that, despite Emmanuel's optimism, it's clear it will be a great deal more expensive than originally planned. This makes the idea of completing the interior of the house as money becomes available particularly appealing. It also means we can complete the entire structural component of the building and drop our half-formed and rather desperate thoughts of building a part-house.

'What a good idea,' I say. 'What a thoroughly good idea. Yes, let's see if we can do that.' Because, at this stage, we're not even sure Council will allow building to lock-up only, or whether among all the rules and regulations – the R-Codes – there's something that prevents owners from inhabiting an unfinished building.

But, oh, how good, how remarkably good, it will be to be in our own place again. The townhouse is perfectly adequate, but it has no soul. And since Richard brought it to my attention, when the breeze is in our direction, the other-worldly howling of the dogs in the Council pound a few streets away enters my dreams as I toss and turn well into the nights.

So far, we have a shortlist of three builders who have expressed interest in this house, all of whom come with solid references and who are willing to consider a contract to lock-up. When they finally supply us with quotes, it turns out there's quite a differential between the lowest and highest with Emmanuel's quotation falling at the high end of in between the two others.

STILL NOTHING HAPPENS

I'm away for six weeks and for four of these I'm in residence at Girton College in Cambridge, England. Each day, I walk across the green fields of what they call "the Backs" to immerse myself in the libraries and archives at Cambridge University as part of my doctoral research. I love every split second of my time in this university city and staying at Girton fulfills something totally inexplicable inside me that I've had ever since I read my mother's precious hardback copy of *The Girton Girl* when I was a young teen. I'm not English, but there's some England in me.

If I'm back at Girton early enough in the evenings, I eat from the extraordinary range of scrumptious buffet dishes in the huge dining room with its soaring ceilings and clerestory windows under the penetrating eyes of the row of past schoolmistresses staring coldly from the paintings along the walls. Other evenings I buy a curry from the restaurant at the bus stop, let myself into the grounds through the latched gate at the back of the campus into the instant hush of a glade of birch trees. In linear time I'm seconds from the main road, seconds from the College, but this place is in between time, a space more real than the real, so silently perfect that an exchange takes place between me and my surroundings, and if my heart beats at all, it beats somewhere outside my body.

In another exchange, I swap coins for a beer from the drinks machine in the corridor and once back in my bare brown-carpeted, brown-blanketed student room I throw up the sash window. And there I sit, sip and eat as the long summer evening flows around me, watching the squirrels and the blackbirds with their so-yellow beaks and thinking how absolutely right Beatrix Potter got this representation of her country.

I go to the student kitchen to get myself a glass of water. Dirty dishes piled everywhere, bin overflowing. As I go to rinse out a glass, a young man using the microwave looks across at me.

'I say, you shouldn't be doing that. Here, let me.' He takes the glass from me. Washes and dries it, mutters to himself, 'You shouldn't see the kitchen like this. Sorry. Terrible mess in here. Pigs, they are. Shouldn't be like this. Sorry, sorry, sorry.' Goes to the fridge. 'Cold water?'

Each morning I get the key from the porter and walk along the tessellated-tile corridors to the long indoor pool which I have all to myself. 'You must be an Australian,' he says when I return. 'It's only the Aussies who use the pool.' In the endless passages of the College, students leap forward to open doors; even a guy on crutches with his leg in plaster insists on opening a door for me.

Sometimes I have lunch in the downstairs dining room of the university's library building. Other times I buy a sandwich and lie by the river under the trees in the Backs and let the summer breezes wash over me. Walking back over the bridge, one of the young men manning the river punts touts for business. They shouldn't make eyes that blue, or mouths that wide with so saucy a grin. Or straw boaters with a ribbon of Cambridge blue to top it all off. How do the girls get any study done?

But the house is never far from my mind and my new surroundings give rise to ideas. I take a lot of snaps. The curvature of the staircase is so elegant, for example, that since Emmanuel convinced us to bring the stairs inside, why not have a curved one? The layout of the courtyard has a Middle Eastern flavour with its long and stately pond and when I see it, I realize that this, too, is part of what we're trying to bring to this home. In a magazine on the flight over, I had seen the ideal arrangement for a breakfast nook or family dining area leading off the kitchen. It would mean extending the house out in a sort of nose, but there was room for it and we could duplicate it on the other side for the study, shortening the verandah, but solving the problem of overlooking the neighbouring house off to the diagonal at the same time.

When Richard comes over, the tempo of my life – and thus my relationship with my environs – changes and my heart thumps to a different tune. But, both at that time and retrospectively, I'm aware that what I experienced, that short period of seamlessness in which I lived, was a privilege. I've never experienced anything quite like it before or since. It was, quite simply, like living in a small bubble out of time. One of life's endless possibilities.

In contrast, Rhodes – where I'm due to present a paper at the Humanities Conference – is dry and treeless, over-hot and bare. When the sun goes down, the tourists spread into the streets like locusts. The waiters are either bored or humourlessly flippant. Or downright rude. They take our orders with eyes rolled to the ceiling or the summer sky, and it's obvious they'd rather be feeding the tourists to the fish than the other way round. If sustainability is the exhortation of the new millennium, I question how sustainable tourism is here. Greece is a series of islands with its soul picked bare. It needs the time it won't get to recover.

Back home, it's obvious from the moment we meet Emmanuel's daughter that she, too, would rather be somewhere else. Since she returned from Sydney, she'd been down to the southwest of Western Australia for a few days which was all too brief, she says, and she's finding it difficult to return to work mode. It's not a terribly good start, but this is a person who's shown a great deal of enthusiasm and empathy on the phone and whom we have been faxing and calling over the past couple of months.

When she shows us her drawings, it's clear she's incorporated the changes we suggested, but other than that they're not a lot different from what we have already. She's done an elevation, too, but it's too modern, encompassing nothing of what we've discussed. And when she suggests a Japanese water feature by the front door, we sense we're not talking quite the same language. We try to point out the features we like in a book of North African courtyards, but she's young and trendy and really can't engage. She takes the book and says she'll go away to have a rethink. Two days later she calls to say she doesn't feel she's the right person for the job.

The problem is we've not only lost another draftsperson and more time, but we've a good chance of losing our preferred builder, too. But then, just because his daughter's ideas don't fit with our own is no real reason to assume that Emmanuel himself is no longer interested. I leave it for a couple of weeks before I take a chance and call his firm. His daughter answers and we chat for a little while before I say, 'We'd still like your Dad to build our house for us. If he's still interested, could he call us?'

When Emmanuel returns my call, he's a little wary, embarrassed perhaps, but yes, he's still interested in the project and recommends a draftsman he's worked with in the past.

We like Murray immediately and once he starts he's quick and efficient. Suddenly, after eight months in the doldrums, we have a fair wind. He appears to understand exactly what it is we want, and two weeks later he has redrawn the plans in more detail than we've had them to date. A week later he presents us with the first set of elevations we've seen that resonates with us.

And then at the end of another week, he's ready for a preview meeting at the Front Counter with the officer handling our plans and the overall chief of the planning department.

Murray calls afterwards, delighted. 'It'll be a breeze now to get it all finalized.' Aside from an adjustment to the level of the car parking area, he says, they're happy with the plans. His voice is thick with satisfaction.

At the end of October, he submits the amended plans to Council. In another six weeks we should have the plans stamped, the building license issued. Too early to celebrate, but enough to get excited about. Although we're a long way from the "lock-up" optimistically pencilled in my diary for the end of this month, at least we're on our way. Our nine months in the rental are up, but we're lucky enough to be able to extend our lease.

I should have learned by now that while a river may look as smooth as a pour of molten silver, under the surface it's still bubbling away. Murray drops in after his next meeting with Council. Furious. Several changes need to be made, but key among them is a requirement that we remove enough soil from the base of the sloping property to pour the bottom slab a metre lower than planned.

'A metre! For heaven's sake.' I do a quick calculation. 'Murray, no! That means half a dozen extra stairs in the staircase which will reduce the space in the downstairs hallway by about a metre and a half. And the ceilings will be four metres high in the flat and the garage area! It's ridiculous. And besides, it'll look silly, too.' It's only after this I remember to ask why.

'I know. It's unworkable,' he says, ignoring my question and dropping into a chair at the dining table while I unroll the drawings once again. 'But it gets worse. Another problem is I'm going away for my annual holiday tomorrow and I won't be back until after Christmas. If only they'd told me this at the Counter weeks ago I could have worked on this then. I went through it in detail with both those guys. I don't understand why they've changed their minds. It'll severely compromise the building. You can't just drop the height like that and I don't have time to talk to them. You'll have to do it.'

'Me? Us? But why…I mean what's the reason they've given for wanting us to drop it?'

'Overlooking the people in front.'

'Overlooking the people *in front*?' I'm mystified. 'But I asked the officer at the Front Counter myself and he said it was overlooking from the side and/or diagonal of a property that concerned them, not the people in front, which seemed cockeyed to me at the time, but…'

He interrupts.

'It's not overlooking from the balcony that worries them; it's overlooking from the garage level.'

'The garage?' I'm mystified. 'But we can't overlook from the garage. There'll be a 2.2 metre limestone wall in the way. Besides who has time to overlook from a garage, driving in and out, unloading the car and so forth…'

'They don't want that either. The wall.'

'What! No boundary wall?'

'Lower. Much lower. Look. Just go along for the meeting. Talk to them and see what's bothering them. Tread carefully. I've seen people dismissed from that office for losing their tempers. Which means you go straight to the bottom of the pile. I'm sorry to leave you with this. I'll see you when I return.'

A few days later we arrive for the meeting with the chief planning officer and his aide and once we're seated in front of him, I can tell you, I'm not thinking Tim Tams. In fact, all our earlier jokes about bribery have a boldness about them that went missing at the door of this office and I wonder, in this instant, what brand of courage – or desperation – it takes to put a bribe on the desk of an official? From the way my stomach is roiling, several bucketloads more than I possess. What we *are* armed with, however, is a good understanding of the current City R-Codes with respect to overlooking, and, as one example of precedent in the same Council jurisdiction, my measurement of the height of the boundary wall between our townhouse rental and the house next door.

Back at home we have a small dog, a longhaired Chihuahua who looks like a miniature collie. When this little chap fronts up to the other dogs in the park, all sniffs and tail wags, he comes across as the friendliest being on the planet. It's not until he has them off-guard that he lunges. Why this picture pops into my mind at this moment, I don't quite know. Perhaps because we're all sitting there smiling and nodding at each other like a row of clowns at a funfair shooting booth.

The chief clears his throat. 'Let's get down to business. Our main worry here is the people in front of you. With these levels you can look right into their yard from your front garden.'

'We plan to build a limestone wall between us…'

'Ah yes, I was coming to that, but now you mention it…that boundary wall.' He moves papers around his desk, finds our specifications. 'The standard height of a boundary wall, as I'm sure you are aware is 1.8 metres. But 2.2 metres is what it says here.' He flicks at the thin line on the plan and the look he gives me over the top of his glasses would fry fish. 'That's a whole 0.4 of a metre – *0.4 of a metre!* – higher than the regulations. Have you…have either of you…any idea what 2.2 metres looks like?'

'Well, yes, actually. Where we're currently living – in the same jurisdiction – we have a partition wall exactly that height that separates us from the townhouse alongside ours and it works very well in terms of privacy for all parties…

'And we've already met with our prospective neighbours to discuss the new wall between our places and swap plans and intentions. In fact, *they* asked for the wall to be this height. I have an email from them to that effect, and we're happy with that because the less overlooking we do is obviously more comfortable for both parties.'

I'm not sure he's heard me as he searches noisily in his top drawer.

'Ah, here it is.' He pulls out a tape and when he stands I'm surprised at how short he is. He takes three strides across his small office to the picture opposite his desk and has several tries at tossing the tape over the frame of the painting. It falls this way and that until is lands across the shoulder of his assistant who has been sitting there silently, looking as though he's just heard he's been posted to Afghanistan. Finally he says to Richard, 'I think you'd better help me with this.' Richard springs to his feet. 'Hook it right up there on top of the frame, will you. That's right. Hold it there while I…' He bends to the floor to take the measurement, snaps upright, flushed and jubilant. 'Ah, yes, thought so! See? 2.2 metres. So that's what your wall is going to look like.

'And let me see…this wall we're talking about, the wall in question… will be only…' Back at his desk he pulls another set of plans in front of him '…about 4 or 5 metres from the sliding doors to your neighbours' family room. How would you like that, eh? How would you like that yourselves? Just think about it. A massive wall looming in front of you?'

'But they asked for it,' I swallow. 'I can provide you with the email from them asking for exactly that,' I repeat.

How is it he's so much larger behind his desk? Seated again, he bends towards me.

'Let's say…let's just say for argument's sake that your neighbours are very *very* nice people and let's just say that perhaps there was some pressure put on them to build a wall that high…'

If I hadn't been forewarned about this interview, something in me would have snapped just then. As it is, I cling hard to the base of my seat and pray to Dad's spirits to keep me in my chair, to keep my face from showing my straight-out indignation. Fury, actually.

Since Richard can usually sense my anger at twenty paces, how can he sit beside me and keep his voice so controlled?

For the next fifteen minutes he reasons with the unreasonable. He talks about the olive trees we're already growing in pots to place along that wall. Trees that will quickly provide mutual privacy for both our neighbours and ourselves from both levels of the house. He talks about all the changes dropping the building by a metre will mean for the plans, the difficulties this will pose to the design, the extra costs in removing soil and building the ground-level walls a metre higher. He discusses the other smaller changes they require. And then he says quietly, 'In the City's R-Codes, it does say that if the height of the wall is agreed between neighbours, Council will consider that height and, if it's not considered unreasonable, approve it.'

Chief of Planning looks at him for a long moment. The aide has his head well down. I can no longer see his face, but he might be meditating. Or praying.

'Ah yes. It might well say that in the current version, but in here…' He brings out a tattered cluster of pages from underneath his keyboard, waves them aloft. 'I still tend to refer to the previous set of codes, you see. And in here it states quite clearly…'

I listen as if in a dream while the man refutes reason based on a set of superseded regulations. When we finally get up to leave, I see two things quite clearly. Firstly, that the charade of measuring the height of the painting down to the floor has been played out in this office many times before. Secondly, that our innocent jokes about bribery have just been swamped by something much darker and more real.

Murray is away for longer than we expect. A lot longer. When I try to call, there's no clue on his answerphone as to when he might be back. In this frustrating break, it's inevitable that, once again, we make changes. But, interestingly, in the way of the universe, it is this further enforced wait and these changes that will make all the difference to the finished house.

One of these is the addition of arcades, three in all, around the internal perimeter of the courtyard which, importantly, will provide undercover access from one part of the house to another.

Another variation is the provision of space for a lift. My father is ninety-six years of age and while he is still capable of tackling stairs, it's a big effort. Other friends of ours are vertically challenged to different degrees. After discussing a number of options, including a wheelchair ramp that would run alongside the outside of the house, we decide the most sensible solution is to make allowance for a lift.

When he returns, Murray charges for each of these changes, but it upsets him, too. Next time we meet to go over the plans, he folds his hands under his chin.

'When we started, you said you were pretty happy with the design and all you needed were working and structural drawings. Instead, I've prepared countless plans moving doors, windows and walls here and there. And now we have all this. This wasn't in the original brief and, quite frankly, I'm annoyed.'

'It's true. I'm sorry. It's just you were away for so long. We had little to do but sit and contemplate. And they're important changes.'

I'm embarrassed. But I appreciate his honesty and straightforwardness, and it makes it easy for both of us to move on with the relationship still intact.

The plans go to Council once again and the pressure is now on us to make final decisions on such items as cornices, pillars and flooring, and what our doors and windows should look like.

Despite negatives like shrinking and swelling with the seasons or, heaven forbid, rotting, we've already decided on wood for the doors and windows. Once Murray has printed out the specifications we trawl through the showrooms of the local timber merchants looking for the right wood. Neither of us is particularly fond of the two local woods usually used for this task: we don't like the colour and heaviness of jarrah or the showiness of marri with its exaggerated veins of dark gum. Nor are we particularly impressed by the finishes of the local product. Or the prices.

We're having a meal one evening at a local café when I realize the folding doors and shutters that lead onto the verandah are exactly what we're after. The colour is a warm and even treacle, the grain is close and not overpowering. I jump up, experiment with closing and opening the doors and they fold smoothly into place.

'What wood is this,' I ask the waiter.

'Teak,' he says. 'The boss imports it.'

As it turns out, in this village-turned-booming-capital, his boss was once my son's boss, too, but there had been a parting of ways that was not entirely painless for my son Viv. And so I am interested for more than one reason to meet this Jonathon.

A short time later, we meet him over an evening meal at one of the restaurants. He's an easy-to-like Indonesian man who tells us that in addition to their restaurant enterprises, he and his brother import wood, either as lengths of timber or custom-produced as doors, windows and shutters. The wood is indeed teak. And, better still, it's recycled.

'All seasoned, so no issue with warping. We collect it from all the old Dutch mansions they're pulling down.'

We show him Murray's specifications of eighteen doors to be made up into three sets of six bifolds, twenty-one internal doors and sixty windows of varying dimensions.

'Can you do this?'

'Yes, no problem. I need the exact sizes first and then I will provide you with a quotation.'

'How long will it take to get here?'

'Ideally, we need a couple of months' notice. A couple of months is all.'

He buys us each a glass of wine, looks at me and asks, 'What is your name again?'

'Tangea Tansley.'

He nods, turns the name over in his mind. And then his head lifts sharply. 'Tansley?'

'Yes, that's right. My son used to work for you. Viv Tansley.'

'Viv? Viv. Viv. You're Vivian's mother?'

'That's right.'

He sits, shaking his head, fiddling with his mobile, and saying Vivian over and over again. For a moment, he's forgotten us. It's clear the disagreement affected him too.

I submit my thesis to examiners on August 12 and the following day we sign up with Emmanuel. It's agreed that the contract will take us to lock-up and we spend some time working out just what this will cover and what it excludes.

I'm about to sign the papers when it dawns on me that today is Friday 13th.

'Friday 13th. Ugh. Is anyone here superstitious?'

The others aren't. I am. You can't grow up in the shadow of a mother who would cross the street to avoid walking under a ladder, toss spilled salt over her left shoulder, avoid looking at the new moon through glass, disallow shoes on tables and the opening of an umbrella in the house, without walking tiptoe through any Friday 13th for the rest of your natural life.

So when I sign my name under Richard's flamboyant signature, I do so a little uneasily. As I've said, building to lock-up means just that: the structural part of the build complete with the external doors and glazing in place so the house can literally be locked up. As a rule of thumb, the finishing from then on represents upwards of about thirty per cent of the cost of the project, so you would imagine there would be an equivalent amount of work the other side of the locked doors. But we didn't fully appreciate at that time quite what that would entail. Or perhaps we knew, but didn't want to see.

Meanwhile, it's one of the realities of suburban infill that we share the lines on the map with no fewer than five neighbouring properties. Why do boundaries turn into problems? Is it our territorial nature? Once we occupy the land within our borders, what happens to ordinary, presumably once-sane humans?

Because we like people and because we hope this project will be blessed with something approaching peace and happiness, it's important to us to get on with our neighbours and we've provided each of the neighbours with a set of our plans. Meanwhile, we already have a good relationship with the folk in front and those on our southern boundary. At least we think so.

It happens first to the north because the owners are all of a sudden ready to pour their limestone driveway and thus in an understandable hurry to discuss the wall between our two properties. We meet on site that evening and agree quite easily that the wall will be limestone. Although we'd prefer natural stone and they want manufactured limestone blocks, we're happy to pay the difference. On the other hand, their site has been cut out of the cliff-side leaving ours hanging above and, according to both the law and the City R-Codes, the onus is on our neighbours to retain where they've made the cut. They agree to pay for the first metre of height if we pay for the next, but from then on it becomes somewhat messy since it's clear that their part of the boundary wall is, in effect, also a retaining wall. We think, however, that we've come to a reasonable compromise and we shake hands.

We get a call from this neighbour one morning soon after to say that the foundations for the wall are going in and if we'd like to check it, we can meet on site after work. When we get there it's raining so hard you'd never guess we have a water problem in this State. The men have already advanced well down the side from the back boundary, slinging blocks into a sloppy furrow. We can't see much and don't want to hang around too long because it's as cold as it is wet, but one thing I can see quite clearly is that the trench is out of alignment.

'Hang on a minute,' I say. 'I think it's out of line with the corner peg back there. It's been built too far over on our land.' Despite their protests, I get a ball of string from the car and run it from one peg to another and it shows the trench they've dug starts nearly half a metre into our block at the top disappearing to zero at the front gate some 80 metres away. Now, that's not a huge triangle of land. But not only are we in the process of losing land that's rightfully ours, we're going to have a side fence that's crooked, too. 'We can't leave it like that.'

'Well, our boundary is right.' Our neighbour-to-be places his hands on his hips. 'We've had it surveyed, too, you know.'

'Yes, yes, of course. I'm sure you have. But if you disagree with ours, where's your peg?'

The limestone workmen keep their heads down, bending low over the channel to heft the heavy stones into place. We're all drenched. Our discussion turns to argument. Although we've had our land recently re-surveyed for the upcoming build, they – husband and wife – maintain they've re-measured theirs 'with a tape' and that it's correct.

I lose my temper, storm off down the driveway, but not before I hear our neighbour-in-waiting say to Richard.

'She's a feisty one, that wife of yours.'

Over the next months, our file of documented evidence mounts. In all, our property is surveyed three times, but in the end we lose out on both counts: we share the cost equally for the wall despite the fact that theirs is largely a retaining wall and we lose land into the bargain. We consult a lawyer who advises we have a good case. But there's so much else to contend with as the build progresses that we give way. So we put the matter to rest by consoling ourselves that, should we wish, we have another twelve years to contest this blatant stealing of land and abrogation of responsibility.

Another problem emerges at the end of the long driveway where the City Codes call for a concrete 'crossover' between drive and road which, given its width, we think would also make a handy temporary car standing given the limited space available in front of the house. We're pacing this out one day when the neighbour in the front house comes out.

She smiles. 'What are you doing?'

'Just measuring for a car-standing space.'

'Car parking? Where?' Her eyebrows shoot up.

'Here…where our crossover widens out. Just a car space, hard standing as it were…'

'There's no room. You can't do it there.' She's genuinely distressed. So are we. We don't want a second neighbour dispute. But they have done exactly what we're proposing alongside their own driveway. I point this out, but she isn't listening.

'But we plan to use this entire front verge as our front garden,' she says, hands on hips. 'We don't want a car blocking the view.'

'It's actually Council land and a Council requirement that we have this area as crossover anyway and it can't possibly block the view any more than a car parked on the roadside outside your house can. And in fact it probably won't be used very often. It's for occasional standing only, for use if someone is delivering something…'

'You can't do it. I'll check with Council.'

Check she does and a letter arrives refusing our application to use part of the crossover as hard-standing. But it goes further than that. If we ignore their injunction, it says, and go ahead regardless, they will bring in concrete-crushing equipment and break up the illegal bay. And why, it finishes up, would we want to spoil our "leafy suburb" by putting in extra concrete anyway?

'But it's not *extra* at all. It's part of their own requirement. How on earth can they say that?' I sit across from Richard. My hands are shaking at the unprovoked hostility of the letter.

'They can do anything they like. And do. It's Council. Councils all over the world are the same.'

'But what about theirs…where they've done exactly what we'd like to do? I don't notice the concrete-crusher doing anything there?'

'If you don't ask and just go ahead and do it, you can get away with most things.'

So, in the interest of holding onto some form of neighbourly relations, we let that go, too.

Because right now, life is challenging on a number of levels and I know I'm out of balance. The fish I've hooked is way too big for me, heading out to sea with me on the other end of the line, and I'm too stubborn or plain stupid to let go of the rod. I go to see my counsellor. I love Jenny for her realness and for the fact that it usually takes no more than a session of her calm insights to set me back on my path. This time she gives me two alternatives, the first being to move.

'Move? To move house? We haven't even moved in yet!' I yelp. I'm appalled at the idea. 'The build hasn't yet started and we have all these problems on the boundaries…'

'The way you describe it, it's the schoolyard bully syndrome. And those people don't stop until they win.'

'They've already won. We wave to each other, but there's an awkwardness. It's horrible.' I can hear the bitterness in my own voice and I'm tempted to add, "The very fact I'm here proves they've won." But I know that's not quite true and that there are other factors involved here, too. This is what happens in Jenny's darkened room with the steady buzz of traffic stopping and starting at the traffic lights outside the window. After just a short while, your mind detaches from your body and looks down at you all scrunched up in the chair, trying hard to unhuddle, unwind, see some sort of light. 'There's no way we could sell the house anyway until it's built. No one wants an abandoned project. We thought we'd have moved in long before now, but instead the slab isn't even down. Besides it's our baby. We…we love it…'

I'm suitably desperate to fully embrace the alternative she puts to me.

'You know, Tangea, all this boundary stuff is just that. It becomes a question of your own personal boundaries,' she says softly. 'If you're determined to stay where you are, then you have to divorce yourself from this project. Pretend it's just that. Just a project and you're the project manager. For the moment, put the love aside. You're letting strangers invade your boundaries and you're too vulnerable. You have other properties, don't you? Well, wear a particular colour of hat for each of those different properties or areas of your life. Edward de Bono's thinking hats. Detach emotionally and when you arrive on site, or in the lecture room, put on the colour hat you've chosen for that particular circumstance and treat it as just another job.'

I have to say that when I finally wobble out of her room into the too-bright day, I wonder at what seems to me to be a rather simplistic solution. I try it out on my visit to the site that evening. As I feel the familiar tightening of my chest, I deliberately breathe more slowly and reach for my hypothetical hat. This one's a cheerful cherry red. I set it carefully on my head. And it works. If I look back at just one skill of the many I gained in building that house, that was an important one. It's a project and I'm there to see it through. It is amazing how much simpler things look after that. The pity is that I don't use this neat aid more often, instead of reaching for it when it's too late.

But it certainly helps with our current problems. We come up with another plan for the crossover area that we duly submit to Council which is finally, although not without opposition, approved. And this is to endow our leafy suburb with more leaf in the form of one of the oldest rose varieties known: the Chinese Mutablis rose which we'll use to hedge the driveway.

THIS IS MEANT TO BE FUN?

All this *matata* – a Swahili word from my East African childhood that roughly translates as fuss – with the slab yet to be poured. I meet the mother of one of my good friends when I'm walking the dogs one day. She is married to one of Perth's early and most successful project builders, so she knows a thing or two about building.

'How is it? Tell me, how's the new house?'

Once I start to tell her, I can't stop. I can't remember exactly what I said. Only the feeling I had at the time: one of tremendous relief at unloading the story of all the difficulties that had beset us, of having a sense that here is someone who would have lived through a daily litany of what can go right or wrong on a build, someone who will surely understand only too well the trials of construction. She listens to me for a while, shakes her head and laughs.

'But building a house…it's meant to be fun!'

Fun?

But shortly afterwards I experience something that convinces me it could be. The building licence is granted two weeks after we signed up with Emmanuel and, true to his word, a week later the bulldozers are on site. That these events are underscored and ringed in red in my diary with so much vigour that the pen has ripped the page testifies as to how central they were to our lives at that time. We've moved on from the bulky file of boundary issues and we have absolute faith in our builder as the foundations for the undercroft are dug and filled with concrete. Thick steel reinforcing rods ring the perimeter of the building. After a shaky lead-up, finally the build is moving along.

'When are the brickies due on site?' I ask Emmanuel.

'Rolf? Rolf should start next week.'

'How many in his team? Do you have an idea how long it will take?'

'Just one. Rolf works alone.'

'What? One brickie. For something this size?' I look up at the reinforcing rods, over three times my height, sticking up out of the hillside. 'How long… how long will he take?'

'Oh, I don't know. He's pretty good.'

Rolf is more than pretty good. He's bloody marvellous, and despite our doubts he's unfazed by the size of the job in front of him. He arrives in his ute each day, self-contained with his sandwich lunch and water, his wheelbarrow and shovel. One of his first jobs is to build the four-metre double-brick reinforced retaining wall that will hold up the main house: over sixteen metres of wall that stretches across the block to stop just short of the sewerage easement and, layer by layer, the intimidating steel rods gradually disappear into tunnels of brick. He mixes his own mud; his questions are gruff and perfunctory; he answers greetings with a grunt. But unlike stories from friends who tell the tale of their double brick walls diverging along their length, Rolf's walls are straight and true. He truly deserves a plaque at the front door, because Rolf built this house, every brick of it. The only trouble is that although he powers along on the days he's there, there are many when he's absent. He's only one man, after all, and when we arrive for a number of evenings in a row to find the site looking sandier and spikier than ever, the ground still sprinkled with haphazardly dumped packs of bricks, it's easy to feel depressed. But in the end, it's not Rolf who holds us up and, in hindsight, we should have worshipped those packs of bricks because the building boom is gathering strength.

It sweeps into our own backyard one day in much the same way the economic crisis did back in the early 2000s, quite gently with just the odd problem showing up here and there like a sudden shoal in smooth water, until the slack tightens between there being no one on site one day and no materials the next. Although we're on a fixed-price contract, that doesn't protect us from delays. And although we aren't directly paying for the price increases ourselves, it doesn't protect us from the escalating tension on the part of our builder.

'Steel prices have doubled in the past year,' he says. 'Bricks are going up. You people are lucky you signed when you did.' He's started calling us 'you people', indicative perhaps of his tension. There's another brick kiln being built in Western Australia, but that doesn't help us or him or anyone else who needs bricks in the present or the immediate future. 'How are you going with the roof tiles? That'll be next. There's a 20 per cent price rise already, and already there are delays.'

We're still waiting to hear about roof tiles. David and Julie return to France each winter, to work physically on a house they're building in the south of the country, and David is trying to source more of the Tegusol colour and profile we've fallen for. The company has stopped making them, but he thinks he knows of an alternative source. He'll let us know in the New Year. Meanwhile, in all our travels around the suburbs, we see nothing we like as much.

It's late November, stinking hot and pouring with rain. Not traditional Perth weather at all on the evening we hold the first of several ceremonies to toast the build. We share the event with Karen and Alex – my daughter Tammy's parents-in-law – who bring along a bottle of Moët and the four of us shelter from most of the downpour under a couple of planks in the lee of what little building there is sipping the bubbly and sharing chilled oysters.

Our feeling of exhilaration has less to do with the champagne and more to do with the close camaraderie of our friends through the tedious beginnings of this build. It has to do with sharing our plans and aggravations and, above all, understanding that although there's not a lot here to celebrate in terms of structure – and although there's more material strewn about the site than there is in the building itself – this moment is huge nonetheless. And absolutely perfect.

Karen clinks glasses, stares out at the mess. 'You're going to have to write about all this, you know,' she says.

In a later ceremony, we will bless the house. But first we gather pieces of our lives together to preserve in a time capsule. The laying of the bottom slab is imminent and our plan is to bury the box of memories in the foundations of the hall. My old teddy bear tops my list. Badly battered through my baby years when I chewed out his glass eyes and bit off his nose – and then further disfigured and dismembered by various unrespecting puppies – Ted is a survivor. With infinite patience, my mother would sew him back together again after each incident until his face was more yellow wool darned in neat crosses than fur and he became so fragile she had to make him pair of blue pyjamas to help hold him together. The bear who has shared so many moves and houses with me deserves to be laid to rest. Because what will happen to him if he outlives me? Which he may well do now the years of his greatest dangers have passed.

I've been through this stuff before. What do you do with other people's treasures when they are no longer around, however much you love the people? What *can* you do with people's treasures? So the box fills with the bear and a few small precious pieces as well as clues that round out this snapshot of lives: our wedding vows, photos of ourselves and our children and a written wish that we hope will hover like a good spirit over the house for all its days. Our wish is that all those who pass over the threshold of this building live out their lives in health and happiness. And then we pack the box with rosemary for remembrance and lavender to keep the pests away. And close the lid.

And now it seems a sound idea to cleanse the site from the dissension that's been attacking its borders: it's time for the blessing.

My brother-in-law Roger is a Reiki master and having done both stages of Reiki with Rog in the past, I'm well aware how powerful a tool it is. So we hold the ceremony standing over the little box in the gaping hole that will one day be a hallway and later Toni and I go to each of the four corners of the property to push sticks of incense into the sand and light them.

Rog and Richard thread a rope through an esky and haul it up the four-metre retaining wall onto what will one day be the main part of the house, but which for the moment is a stretch of well-packed sand. We lay down a picnic rug and surround it with half a dozen little citronella lamps – for light and to keep away the mozzies – and then we tuck into our feast of spicy roast chicken, prawns and salads and wash it down with champagne.

For the first time the extent and limit of our view is no longer a tease. We now know we'll get a very satisfying river vista. Even if I stand at the back of the house – in the gallery space – despite the predictions of the experts to the contrary, we have an uninterrupted view out across the water to the houses clustered on the opposite shore. As we lie back on the sand in what will be the courtyard, there are stars piercing the gentle dark above us, lights flickering on around the far river bank, the sound of birds turning in for the night. What can I say?

The December/January builder's break comes. Again. The difference this time is that the first of five lump sum payments is credited to the builder's account. We've been in the rental for 18 months – the property bulls are running full tilt – and it's at this point we start to wonder whether it would have been wiser, financially, to have held onto the Lockhart Street house. Meanwhile, Rolf's ute is nowhere to be seen with nothing at all happening on site. We paint the huge and ugly dark brown brick of the retaining wall that runs along one side of the plot in dark green but it looks worse. With my son Viv's help, we paint it again until it's a relatively unconfronting sage.

The waiting is getting us down and it feels good to be doing something. Anything. I take Richard up to Broome in the North West of the State for his birthday weekend and it's disastrous. Out of season, the town steams in midsummer heat and we steam along with it. It's a relief to fly back home.

It's 2005, nearly five years after the planning weekends that started us off on this trajectory. Perhaps it's time for a review. Or another plan. To relieve his frustration Richard builds a model of our house-in-waiting out of balsa wood. He sets out the block with all its idiosyncratic heights, boundaries and retaining walls, cuts up one of the stack of plans mounting at one end of the dining table and builds the small structure to scale with all its arches, pillars, arcades and courtyard. He debates what material to use for the roof, discards my suggestions of balsa or cardboard or anything really. So, for the moment it's a house without a roof, but at least I can see what it will look like when it's built. I mentally colour it my favourite pale yellow, paint in geraniums cascading over the balcony, trees to soften the edges and give it a driveway in rust-red brick.

If you didn't know better, you'd think there was nothing romantic about a huge Readymix concrete mixer standing on the empty block above ours with its drum slowly revolving and a thick rubber hose stretching down the hill towards us. But when you've waited so long, staring enviously at these very trucks passing on their way to other jobs while keeping your fingers and toes crossed that the cement shortages they're foretelling are but media myth, the sight of the yellow-and-white monster this steamy March morning is heart-stoppingly lovely.

And when the snaking hose rears up and all that grey sludge starts to pour out, grudgingly at first, until it's a long thick stream and your eyes start tearing when there's absolutely nothing to cry about, it's the closest thing I know to meeting your child for the first time. I know without looking that Richard is similarly affected. Our builder runs from one end of the site to the other, shouting instructions at the four men in Wellington books pushing and raking the concrete. The site is all movement and focus. Emmanuel is in his element and we all exchange smiles of satisfaction.

How good it looks when it's down, glinting wetly in the sun, surrounding the sandpit in the middle which will one day – gradually getting closer – be green and lush.

It's hard to leave all this to go off for the day's lecturing.

Once Rolf is back, the stacks of bricks dissolve into walls, but before long we're forced to accept that the statewide shortage of bricks is a reality and that the rival kiln being built is not going to help. The bigger builders have the ability to stockpile, not so the smaller ones. A pile of bricks sitting on someone's lonely verge with the grass growing up around the base is a joke until my thinking changes to the point where I wonder whether they actually need those bricks. Although reason tells me that all the odd piles of bricks in the whole of the world aren't going to be enough to finish this house, reason doesn't have the upper hand at the moment.

But now at least we can see what's what and we can start measuring. And, aside from a mistake in the width of the slab in the bedroom, which Emmanuel assures us is easily fixed, the structure so far can't be faulted.

The scarcity of bricks is one problem, the other remains the roof tiles. We still haven't heard anything definitive from David. We know only that the tiles are in full production overseas, but the delay in delivery has stretched out to three months. At the moment, Emmanuel is not pressing us for a decision, but he does bring up a very good point: if it turns out that we *are* able to get our tiles from France, who is going to lay them? Somehow we had thought this Emmanuel's responsibility, but not it seems, if the tiles are owner-sourced. Another of our key lessons: check the fine print. Problems tend to arise from the omissions in a contract rather than the inclusions.

Back to the yellow pages which, in this instance, are no help at all. It seems that all the roof tilers in the State are employed by the tile companies. Don't lone operators exist in this industry? And this leads me to a piece of logic that evidently passed me by earlier. It figures that if all the tiles in the State are being laid as fast as they're being manufactured, all available tilers are going to be flat out laying those tiles. I think Emmanuel had already warned me of this, but I'm not sure I took it in. I leave him calls that don't get returned and wonder what we're going to do. One solution we quickly discard is to do it ourselves. I don't think roof tiling can be any more difficult than anything else we've tackled, but the idea of being that high off the ground is terrifying.

They call it "a flood of relief" because that's what it's like – a wall of water thundering down a sandy river bed – the day David phones.

'The tiles are on their way. They should be here within a month, cleared and through customs a week after that. So, say five weeks all up, maybe sooner.'

'Thank God. That's marvellous.' My words are fervent. Not only have we (almost) got the tiles we wanted, but with the recent price rises, they work out cheaper than the local tiles. What's more, they'll be here just when they're needed, several months earlier than we would have been able to get hold of local ones. It's now March, they'll be here in April. It seems too good to be true. I can call Emmanuel to tell him the news. I bask for exactly a second in this wave of fortune until reality catches up. My brain flashes red and yellow signals. Without a tiler, we're still stuck. Or worse. Now we're committed to a roof's worth of tiles that we'll certainly have to take delivery of. With no tiler to lay them. I take a deep breath.

'David, I think we've got a bit of a problem…a huge problem actually… Any idea where we can get hold of a tiler? I've tried calling all over, but so far…'

'Tiler? These tiles come with a tiler. Didn't I mention that? In fact they come with the best tiler in the business. John, his name is. He's worked for me for years. It's all in the price I quoted you.'

Why hadn't I thought of that? What hadn't I thought to ask David in the first place? I think that's what happens when you're under pressure.

You act like a rat on a wheel, tackling only what's in front of you and totally forgetting to look sideways.

In a bid for balance, we take up yoga. Our instructor is as friendly as she is lithe, a good teacher, encouraging with a gentle sense of humour. At first Richard is the only male in the class and then over the next weeks two or three other men join in. The impossible bends and stretches help, but it's the ten minutes' meditation at the end we find most beneficial.

I used to meditate. Why did I drop it? Meditation gives you that precious time to stand back and look at yourself, to examine the self-talk and dismiss the negative for what it is. It gives you a chance to stop the world whirling. How difficult it is to be human. I'm not sure whether Richard is meditating or resting. I lie within arm's stretch so I can nudge him when he starts to snore. Which he does each time after a couple of minutes. How I envy someone who can drop off to sleep so easily.

We buy a little green goddess that we place gingerly on the balcony of the balsa wood house. Each evening from then on until we move into the brick version, we light a stick of incense which the tiny goddess holds while the smoke spirals over the model.

The irritating thing about the raft of sudden decisions we now face is that although over the past couple of years we've worked through a lot of them, in the time that has elapsed many of the products have been superseded or are simply no longer available and many of the "handy" phone numbers stockpiled so rigorously are dead and gone.

It wasn't quite clear to us at the time how thoroughly change was making itself felt. It never is when you're in the thick of things, but the Western Australian economy was shooting away from us and all we could do was try to keep our balance. Nothing to hang on to. Like riding a bike without handlebars. Or skateboarding down a steep hill.

So even though we're deliberately setting out to build an untrendy house that won't date with the whim of the market, we are to a certain extent trapped by trend. It's like trying to buy a fitted pencil skirt when A-lines are all the fashion. Or finding white in winter, black in summer. Or trying to sell a modern house without a dishwasher.

The bigger picture is even more alarming. It seems quite ludicrous we were once actually stupid enough to contemplate building a house exactly the right size for our future needs. Had we built our one-bedroom home in this location – surrounded on all sides by large houses – we would have achieved a white elephant on a hillside. It would have been unique all right, so unique that it would have been unsaleable. When I first came to Australia, it was more usual to have the dunny or toilet in the back garden than inside the house. Now two bathrooms are the norm and a house doesn't have to be a mansion to contain as many as five. All this in such a comparatively short space of time.

Flooring is high on the list of current decisions. The first part is simple. Of the main choices – carpet, timber or tile – tile is an easy winner. We both like it; it's cool in summer, retains the heat in winter, easy to take care of in terms of spills and general cleaning and suits the type of house we're building. I love the thought of tiled arcades set against what will one day – please God – be the lush green of the courtyard, and a picture of the dogs hauling themselves drowsily from sun to shade and back again is never far from my mind. Tile says hot countries, cool against bare feet, and has a sort of holiday spirit about it. Holiday? Hmm…

When we set out to do our homework on tiles, we do so with two reservations: its potential slipperiness and the pain of maintaining the cleanliness of the grout. We decide the way around these two negatives is to choose unglazed tiles and minimize the width of the grout. We soon learn that what we're after are what they call "rectified" tiles with sharp square edges which use considerably less grout than those slightly rounded. We search through the tiling shops and bring home boot loads of samples, lay them out on the townhouse balcony, and live with the decision for a couple of weeks. We're just about to make a decision when we go to a Home Open and see these same tiles on the floor for real. I catch Richard's gaze and know he's thinking the same thing: Oops! *En masse*, they don't look good, in fact, their smooth blandness is overwhelmingly depressing. Because we plan to tile the entire house – over 400 square metres – we can't afford to make a mistake. Either aesthetically or financially. We start at the beginning again.

This could have gone on for a while, but we're visiting my cousin in East Perth one day when we notice an Indonesian importer has set up shop at the end of the street. In his window he has a selection of marble tiles.

Marble is not a surface we've contemplated. It reminds me of those photos in the glossies where the floors look as treacherous as a skating rink, cold, almost inhuman, far from the atmosphere we're trying to create. But this is marble with a difference. It comes from Indonesia and while some of the sample tiles are too heavily veined for our liking, there are two – a cream with terracotta veins and a terracotta with cream veins – we take a liking to. Tiles will always be slippery when wet – timber, too, for that matter – but if we buy them "honed" or unpolished, we're told, that problem is considerably lessened. So we take home two samples, the cream and the terracotta, thinking at first that they may be suitable for the bathrooms.

When we place them on the floor, we start to fall so completely in love with them we consider using the cream ones for the whole house. 'And the colours complement each other so beautifully we could lay them on the diagonal in the arcades,' Richard says. It sounds so instantly right that my mind's eye takes off along these outside corridors where the terracotta and cream are laid alternately and on the diagonal so the squares become diamonds.

Meanwhile the consignment of doors and windows has arrived together with the dozens of planks of recycled wood that Richard plans to use for the built-in furniture. There are piles of internal doors, door jambs and windows, as well as three sets of bifolds, each door of which is designed to hold eight panes of glass. This house is as much glass as it is brick and tile. But Jonathan has done us proud. Not only has he supplied the goods when he said he would, but the teak is beautiful, all recycled and therefore well-seasoned with a tight grain and a rich warm honeyed colour. What's more, to Rolf's relief, our prayers and Emmanuel's surprise, they all fit perfectly.

But all this timber needs treating which calls for our first serious assault on the major Australia and New Zealand hardware chain, Bunnings. In recent times, it's seemed everyone we meet is an expert on how best to treat wood: we've received more advice on wood finishes than on any other single element of this house. Now, standing in the middle of the warehouse aisle, dwarfed by shelf after shelf of a disquieting selection of wood oils, varnishes and various finishes, I can see why. There's lots of it, that's why.

We had been advised to use a product called Sikkens by one of the local door manufacturers although another had said we'd be inviting trouble if we went that way. Jonathan insists that all he's used on his restaurant doors is oil.

'But which oil?' I remember oiling the jarrah boundary fence at my cottage in North Fremantle. 'Like linseed? There are dozens…'

'No, not linseed. Oil, just oil, you know. It's the best. Believe me.' He's as adamant as he is vague.

The only thing we're reasonably clear on is that we don't want to use a polyurethane product because of the necessity to strip it right back when it starts to deteriorate, as deteriorate it will with time and sun. As carpenter's mate, inevitably most of the sanding will fall to me, and sanding back any flaking finish – be it paint or varnish – comes at the top of the list of my least favourite jobs. Hopefully, oil will require less upkeep.

THIS IS MEANT TO BE FUN?

So we start off by using a straightforward decking oil. It changes the colour of the teak a little, instead of honey we have syrup, but the timber comes up sleek and smooth.

Deliberately we have avoided any windows on the hot west-facing aspect of the gallery and have only one back door leading to what will become the drying green and fruit and vegetable garden, and on this we use a strong marine polyurethane varnish.

Oiling the wood becomes a nightly task for the next couple of weeks as we strive to keep up with Rolf who's starting to put the door and window frames in place. Once it gets dark on site, we take the myriads of glazing bars back to the garage in the townhouse to continue under the garage lights well into the night.

One evening we are brushing away on the front lawn when a stranger stops to chat.

'That's teak, isn't it? Thought as much. Smell it from half a mile away. I'm a boat builder by trade and that's the timber we always use.' He picks up a length of wood, runs his hands slowly across the grain. 'Lovely to work with and by far and away the gutsiest wood in the world.'

We're lucky in that our consignment of the gutsiest wood in the world has been so well-prepared it hardly needs sanding and gradually the pile of treated frames outpaces Rolf.

Being an internal site, locked in by other houses, space was always going to be a problem on this block of land and, from the start, it's an untidy building site. The pile of yellow sand dumped at the entrance makes coming and going a challenge and immovable packs of bricks and bags of cement are dotted about haphazardly without a thought for the other materials to follow. So with the progressive arrival of the mobile toilet, the reinforcing rods, roofing timbers, tiles, gutters, downpipes and the enormous rolled-steel joists, there's little room to move. For the moment, the owner-purchased items like door and windows have to be placed on the sandy floor of what will be the garage. Later we spend a couple of hours carrying each of the heavy solid-wood doors up the concrete stairs to what will be the gallery, stack them in a neat pile in the centre of the floor, out of the way of the plasterers who'll be coming as soon as we have a roof. Emmanuel is furious.

'Not like that. Stand them up. Stand them up. Otherwise they'll warp.' So we heft them upright.

But it's not only the thoughtless way the building materials have been offloaded that clogs up the site. It's the accumulating rubbish, too. Rolf is economical in that there's only him. He mixes his own mortar, locks up his barrow at the end of the day and takes his lunch wraps home with him. But not so the others. When the other tradesmen arrive, they drop everything right where they're sitting or standing. Like *everything*. Half-eaten sandwiches and burgers, Coke bottles, pizza containers, cigarette butts and empty packets. And as for plastic: we could fill a skip with the endless water bottles and plastic bags. The fallout from the lunches alone is enough to move this planet one giant step closer to its finale. I'd tackled Emmanuel early on about the empty food and drink containers, but he'd shrugged.

'Tradesmen. They're all the same.'

But it's not only food and drink containers. It's broken bricks, half bricks, brick ties and strips of plastic. And then, progressively, offcuts of wood from the roofing timbers, nails, jagged bits of steel, broken glass, reinforcing rods, endless lengths and snips of electrical wire, conduit and bits of piping. It bothers us, this increasing mess, and we take to picking it up each evening and placing it on a growing pile. For the dogs, however, a visit to the site (any site) is paradise. Zorro – fighter extraordinaire and fearless walker of walls – makes straight for the pile each evening and balances on the growing heap, sorting through scrunched-up paper and plastic until it's time for home. Not good for his waistline, but rather Zorro than the rats I think. When rats get a hold, they're hard to beat. And we'll be living by the river. In the end, though, it defeats us all. A huge pile of everything, a lot of which should be recycled and much of it, surely, still usable? Bricks with a chip off the corner can disappear under plaster; half-tiles can still make quarter-tiles. Having been brought up in a waste-not, want-not family, I find it hard to believe such waste. Once again, I approach Emmanuel.

'It's not only a mess: it's dangerous too, with all the ribbons of sliced steel and nails.' It's been some nights since we picked up the rubbish and the site's reverted to a tip once more. I gesture around me.

'I'll get it cleaned up tomorrow,' he promises.

'And would you get a skip? Can't we get rid of that pile?'

He's standing on the balcony, gazing out over the rubbish, with a strange look on his face. It's hard to fathom, that look. Almost, but not quite, one of satisfaction. 'What? That little heap. It's not big enough yet.'

I persist. 'There's a skip's worth there, surely?'

'Oh no. Not yet.' And then something clicks and I recognize the look. It's one I'm sure I wear myself when I figure I can get two meals out of one dish.

Two weeks later, the pile is taller than me. Besides, it's time to install the limestone steps alongside the house up to the back garden. I've promised our contractor Dave, who's done a number of jobs for us over the last couple of years, that the way will be clear for him to work. I ask Emmanuel if he would mind either moving or removing the pile of rubble.

'But he'll be bringing the blocks on a bulldozer, won't he? Well, he can move the pile out of the way at the same time.'

'But I said we'd clear…' I start.

'Oh, it's nothing. Once he has the machine there, it'll take him only two minutes to move that lot out of the way.'

I give way to his experience.

But, next day, Dave isn't happy when I ask. Understandably. I had promised him a clear path and it's not his job to move rubbish about. After all, he has a day of hefting giant blocks ahead of him. He doesn't say anything, but I can tell from the jerky energy with which he swings the big machine back and forth that he's furious.

I have a dream in which the house is finished and I'm proudly showing friends around. Everything is so perfect. The walls are plastered and painted, the stainless steel bathroom fittings gleam, the bifolds slide back with ease, the arcades are just as I imagined. My mother taps me on the shoulder. Pride comes before a fall, she says, just as there's a thunderclap and the rain sheets down. There's no time to run for cover and we're all drenched. Even in my dream, I question this 'running for cover' since we're inside the house, but then I look up and see the building still lacks a roof.

The next day the dream is still vivid, keeps nagging at my mind. Dreams about water usually foretell there's a heavy expenditure of emotion on the way: if the water is clear it will be a positive emotion. But if it's murky, that's not usually such good news. My dream rain was somewhere in between: it wasn't clear, but it was not exactly cloudy either, both transparent and silvery at the same time. When I visit the site that evening, there's real rain gushing down the concrete stairs. 'A natural water feature,' I joke, but I'm uneasy. The dream is too real and I just want the roof on and the project finished.

But now there's a three-week delay in roofing carpenters. Our tiles have arrived on time; we have a window of opportunity with our tiler who is booked for the following month, but so far no timbers on which to lay them.

Just as we fix one problem, another arises. For the first time I think back to the day we signed the contract: Friday 13th.

It was Richard's idea that one way to save a clear, after-tax, very useful sum of around $50,000 would be to paint the house ourselves. Now, I've painted plenty of single rooms over my lifetime. I also painted my cottage (over time) and one of the children's investment flats. But a whole house? At least half of which is double-storey?

To boot, there's a communication glitch between us. Initially, it's not clear to me that by 'paint the house' Richard means the whole house – both inside and out, naturally to him and not-so-naturally to me – so I get sort of sucked in. Not exactly unwilling, more like unwitting.

The walls are up, ready for the outside render before painting, but Emmanuel's usual plasterers have moved to the north of the State where there's a resources boom and he's having to source another team. So we can't start painting yet. But in the interim, another paint job we hadn't anticipated needs attention. The scaffolding is up and the roof timbers have finally been completed by a couple of fairly rough and ready carpenters, and, quite suddenly, the half-metre lengths of exposed rafters along the front of the house and partly along the sides of the building need sealing or painting or both, before the roof goes on. The tiler – our tiler, the one available roof tiler in the whole of Western Australia – is scheduled to start the following Monday, less than a week away. 'I know a great team,' our builder says. 'Two Turkish painters. They'll knock off those rafters in a weekend, easy. I can get a quote.'

Shading my eyes from the sun, I look up at the rafters eight metres above us, and the proportion of my height to the building is such that I wonder whether this is what it feels like to be a Chihuahua at the foot of a Great Dane.

I drive home, thoughts buzzing. This is yet more money we hadn't anticipated going out. Most things we do ourselves, but I've never worked on scaffolding. I'm not terrified of heights, but not exactly keen on them either. And that scaffolding looks about as dicey as the squares of trussed-up bamboo poles the building teams use to swarm up twenty or forty or sixty floors above the ground in Hong Kong. There's a bit of a tussle going on Tangea to Tangea. I've never been a person who states *I don't do this or that*: I like to think I'll have a go at anything. But here's an exception. It's a long way off the ground, that roof. By the time my husband comes home, my mind is made up.

'Emmanuel has mentioned a Turkish painting team who'll give us a reasonable price. Let's get them to do the rafters,' I say. 'It's really not something I want to do…'

From his ready agreement, I figure he's no keener than me. He nods. 'We don't have a lot of time to waste with the tiler due on Monday. It's got to be done before then. See how quickly you can get a quote.'

The quotation comes through from Emmanuel several days later on Friday afternoon at 3.30 p.m. It would take a day, the Turkish team estimates, and the cost would be $3,500. Including service tax, they add generously.

An unwillingness to spend a sum of $3,500 on a day's work coupled with the only available tiler in the State set to turn up the other side of the weekend constitutes enough of a crisis to change my mindset rather radically. I call Richard.

'How about I pop up to Bunnings and get some paint? Let's have a go?'

This is the first lot of paint we've bought for this build and the check out docket is as clear in my mind as it was the day it was handed to me: all of $115 worth of primer, paint and brushes.

We arrive on site early on the Saturday morning and it's a bit like the stories you hear about painting the Sydney Harbour Bridge: the primer is dry enough for the first coat of Dulux by the time we get back to the beginning again. And yes, the scaffolding is downright scary in that some of it lacks a safety railing and has shoe-width gaps in the narrow planks, a real trap when your attention is necessarily focused upwards. Even more terrifying is swinging onto it from a ladder on the balcony. I sprawl across the planks, my husband gives my bottom an extra heft and I'm up. Up… and trying not to look down.

I'm not exactly shaking with fear, but I don't feel very stable either. A bit shivery and ephemeral as if all my flesh and blood has shrivelled up and left the bones to get on with the job. Richard manages much better than I do, partly because he's stronger and has greater reach, but mainly I suspect because he has the strength of mind to ignore the mass of broken bricks and splintered steel some six metres below. Being the wimp I am, it turns out it's easier to stay up there all day than face the trauma of clambering back down onto the slab. So I'm handed a thermos of black tea and plenty of water. Holding tightly to the outside rail with one hand, I set my teeth and bend to stir the paint pot. Richard starts on the other side of the building and bit by bit we cover the wood.

I even eat my lunch up there sitting cross-legged on the boards under a sky so blue you'd never think it midwinter. And I wonder why it's taken this particular job to give me time to actually appreciate where I'm going to live. To stop for long enough to enjoy the bird life perching among the flamboyant streamers of bougainvillea blossoms that tumble over our neighbour's huge wall. The honeyeaters searching for spider treats, the willie-wagtails bossing the doves, the crows competing for attention, and out on the river, pelicans massing for a feed. The water, though, is the greatest distraction, splattered as it is with greys and blues and flecks of silver, a twenty-first-century Van Gogh painting on which a handful of yachts and windsurfers beg for a breeze that even up here is so slight it fails to make the papery bougainvillea bracts dance. A more than fair exchange, all this gentle beauty for my earlier terror.

The problem with experiencing perfection is that it contains some sort of pheromone that challenges the senses to improve upon it. Partly to distract my mind from my bladder, I start to think we could have a roof garden up here: it would still be within the height restriction and it wouldn't be difficult to add a spiral staircase to one end of the balcony. Thankfully, the thought of going back through Council – ever – stops my thoughts right there. It's enough, though, to break my lazy spell, and I haul myself to my feet.

We complete the job the following day, on a Sunday morning with enough time to spare to meet our friends for lunch. One and a half days it has taken us to put a primer and two topcoats on those rafters and we've saved ourselves a precious $3,500...less the tiny sum of $115.

EXPENDABLE GRANDMOTHERS

John, the roof tiler, a loose-limbed straightforward sort of a chap in his early sixties who walks with a limp and says what he thinks, is the complete opposite to the quick-moving and urbane Emmanuel. I'm there on site to make the introduction and it's perfectly clear they loathe each other on sight.

We're strolling across the top slab ostensibly to familiarise John with the building he's going to be working on for the next month, but from the body language both men display I get the feeling there's something else going on.

This is Emmanuel's site until he hands it over. That had been made clear to us from the start. But, months back, when we first discussed the possibility of bringing over our own tiles, he didn't appear to be unhappy about the idea. And now we actually have a tiler, the roof brings him a twofold advantage in that not only does he avoid the twenty per cent price rise in local roof tiles, but it also circumvents the escalating delays in supply. As well, the tiling can now start in May where it would otherwise have had to wait until much later in the year.

But now, as I listen to them, I'm aware that our builder's usual clear reasoning is awash with something over which logic has no control. An undercurrent of primal territorialism. Boundaries again. John is questioning Emmanuel, who answers reluctantly. But it's John's muttered, 'I thought as much. No foresight,' that does it, and the men veer away from each other with the slippery finesse of two amoebas. Emmanuel makes it clear how he feels in a phone call later that day. 'I don't get on with that guy. Let him do his job and then get off my site. I'm not going to the house while he's there.'

Soothing doesn't help. He's adamant. His feelings have been wounded and his pride is at stake. I can see his point of view, but there's nothing we can do.

John wants a hoist. We're standing among the rubble on the lower level and he's squinting into the sky.

'How on earth did the brickies get their stuff up there?'

'Rolf, you mean? He carried his bricks. Half a dozen at a time…'

'Well, I'm not doing it that way. Impossible. Take three times as long. I need a hoist. Didn't David tell you?'

David might have, I can't remember. But there's more.

'I'm also going to need more sarking, the waterproof sheeting that goes under the tiles. Somewhere along the line there's been a miscalculation…'

The balcony roof, too, is an anomaly since the slope is only four or five per cent while at least sixteen per cent is required for adequate water run-off. Even the main roof only just qualifies in this respect. The draftsman had wanted to use corrugated iron over the balcony, but we couldn't see a happy marriage between tin and tile. 'You won't see it,' he'd said. But we have been persuaded so often in the last few months to go against our gut feeling for another's convenience that we opt for David's solution to the problem: a slightly different profile of tile, with a thick sheeting of Hardiboard underneath.

But at last, at long last, we're getting a roof. No more food for the demons of my waking dream of a roofless house.

Each day the list of difficulties gets longer. The solar hot water system we wanted is proving unviable from both a financial and design point of view. We meet with representatives of the three firms currently offering this product in Western Australia, but no matter how many times we do the sums, even with the government rebate, it will take about twenty years to break even, by which time the unit itself will need replacing. And although we have the perfect north northwest roof for optimum heat, the design of the house with the downstairs flat proves to be a problem.

It's disappointing. All the sun we have in this country and we still can't get it right. I remember flying into Rhodes for a conference where almost all flat Greek rooftops sported solar hot-water tanks. In fact, both apartments and hotels had quite a bevy of them snuggled side-by-side and in most places we stayed this was the premier method of heating water.

In the meantime, our fallback position is gas, but we can't have the gas hot water system we want because the gas supply to this area, for a reason no one can adequately explain, lacks the necessary pressure. We end up with no choice but to go with two standard gas-fired hot water heaters. There's a 10-year warranty on these heaters and I know from experience they'll need replacing in exactly 10 years and one day. Built-in obsolescence where the sacrificial node in each will rust through to order.

No chemical-free termite protection. No solar hot water. How difficult can it be to eco-build?

We go to yoga, breathe, meditate, and stretch. Take up tai chi to concentrate on very little. We need this.

My sister Toni calls and leaves a message.

'Tange, do you want gates for the new house? There are some advertised in this week's *Post*. They sound nice.' She leaves a phone number and rings off.

I groan to Richard. 'Gates? The absolutely very last thing on my mind right now. We're miles away from needing them.'

'Call up. See what they're like.'

From the photo emailed to us, they look more than nice. They look great. And tall enough to complement the height of the house. We drive up to a property in the hills and buy them with half the money that would have gone to the Turkish painters. They'll be delivered the following week. Onto a site that already has no space to move.

Meanwhile, since Emmanuel still hasn't come up with a plastering team, our next paint job is the exposed rafters that sit under the tiles in the courtyard. The courtyard – that clear and vibrant picture of spiritual green and fragrant blossom I hold somewhere close to my soul – is so far away right now that I wonder at our foolishness for injecting this square of hot sand into the middle of the house. Actually, it's not even sand. The mounting rubble is as much a problem up here as it is on the rest of the block. Despite our continuing efforts to clean it up, the site still looks like a rubbish dump, and it's difficult to move from one end to another without twisting an ankle. All along, Emmanuel has been reluctant to clean up and it's beginning to get to us both.

But it's not the fault of the untidy site, but of the ladder – our own ladder – that collapses quite suddenly under Richard that causes the next problem. Although it certainly doesn't help that he falls awkwardly on broken brick.

Are the next days a nightmare? I don't know…they whip past like film tape out of control and it's only in looking back I remember anything at all. Although he was shaken at the time of the fall, he seemed all right until a few days later when he woke screaming in pain. His doctor of the past twenty years is miffed we've moved to the next suburb and decides, therefore, that he can't visit him 'because he's out of my area', but he can call an ambulance. When they arrive at the townhouse, the two ambulance officers take one look at Richard's prone body and say they'll need help to carry him down the stairs.

We're lucky there are Council workers lopping peppermint trees just up the street and they're co-opted for the job almost before they know it. Four large men in ripped t-shirts and heavy boots, not quite knowing where to look as they shuffle into our bedroom. But they're strong and efficient. What I remember most clearly just as Richard is shunted into the ambulance is one man, a huge Rastafarian with dreadlocks and a shirt that has more rents than it does cloth, setting his side of the stretcher down so softly it might have contained a sickly child.

'I sure hope you get better,' he says looking into Richard's face which is by now a cast of pain. He squeezes my husband's shoulder, his voice gruff. 'That's like, you goin' to get better, man. You goin' to get better. Hear?'

With such good vibes, how could he not? In fact after two days in hospital and another couple at home, he's back at the office during the day…and back at work at night.

But with Richard out of action the day the gates arrive, there's only Rolf who kindly agrees to help the deliveryman and me get those impossibly heavy gates off the trailer. The three of us bend our knees, grit our teeth and by the sort of effort fuelled by something beyond our own strength somehow half-lift, half-drag them up against the garden wall. Where, for the next six months, they're always in the way and moved with great difficulty, and then moved again, from place to inconvenient place. But when they're finally up, they're splendid.

So are the roof tiles. Once we get John his hoist, like Rolf, he is his own team. Silhouetted against the sky, the gait that had been ungainly on the ground turns to ballet as he steps lightly from joist to joist and, later as the tiles are slotted into place, balances firmly on the sloping roof itself. The roof in Applecross that had been the inspiration for ours and thus the contact with David and John – has lost a portion of its tiling in a recent storm. When I mention this to John, he assures me that he nails every second tile, so it will take more than a storm to shift ours.

'Withstand a bloody cyclone, the way this lot are laid. You've no worries about that.'

He's interested in Richard's unreliable ladder that we've consigned to the garbage heap until I tell him why it's there.

'Fell off a ladder, m'self, a couple or three months back. Got careless and it reared back on me. Went over backwards and fell flat on my back with my butt taking most of the weight. My bum's still black with the bruising. Lucky not to break something.

'What colour do you want the cement for the ridge tiles? There's no exact match for this particular tile, but I recommend you go darker rather than lighter with the grout because it'll fade where your tiles won't.'

Even as the work progresses towards its finale, we've more than enough packs of tile competing for storage space in the cramped front garden. It becomes clear that David has over-calculated the number we need. And then, literally overnight, there are only a handful left: twelve tiles that John recommends we bury in the garden for use in the event of breakages. If indeed the remainder went anywhere, I can only hope they were used to re-tile the roof of the house that was such a happy inspiration for us.

The roof is most visible from the courtyard. And the tiles are perfect for this house.

For kitchens, stone is the 'in' material right now and here we're happy to go with trend. Granite, marble, limestone, sandstone, riverstone and the "manufactured stone" of Caesarstone, terrazzo and the like. There's a wealth of colours, quality and amalgams to choose from. Again the choices are infinite and overwhelming.

I'd like to get the kitchen designed – and equipped – by an experienced kitchen company. Actually, a bit more than like. There's a bit of dreaming attached to this, too. Imagine just going in and asking someone to translate your wants and wishes into a real live smart-looking workspace? But Richard has other ideas. After visiting showroom after showroom and exploring every cabinet maker in town, he's adamant he's going to fit out the kitchen himself He's already started making the bases and plans to buy flatpack cupboards from Ikea, assemble them himself and make the templates for whatever countertop material we decide on.

'Do the kitchen ourselves? With everything else we have on? The painting'll be coming up any tick of the clock. And Ikea cabinets?' I'm dubious. No, more than dubious: I'm downright glum. Ikea has solved many a problem for me over the years, but I don't like cabinets with holes down the sides. Practical, I know, but not aesthetic. We've put so much into this house it seems silly to spoil it by overlooking the detail. And it's the quality of the finishes that make a project, any project, look good. Or bad. We've said that all along.

'We can cover the holes with iron-on strips,' Richard says. 'Stop stressing, for God's sake.'

Am I stressing? What's happening to me? What's amiss that I even notice a row of little holes in cabinet walls? Something I can ask, but not answer.

We're snapping a lot at each other now, I note. Something to do with lack of sleep? Or the howling from the pound down the road that travels along the winding roads of my dreams? Or Perth's entire bird population that congregates in the ghost gums across the road and makes merry in the long hour before dawn? Or is it just the nature of building this way with not quite enough money and a build that's constantly evolving? With all the stops and starts? I remember showing our early house plans to Richard's mother and his sister Jenny back in the UK. I can't remember Jenny's exact words, but something about the strain of building and was I sure I was up to it? Back then, I wondered what she was on about.

That night, a hand moves across the bed, finds mine, and we clasp tight.

There's been a delay in the delivery of the gutters and downpipes which, when they finally arrive, turn out to be the round profile instead of the square ones we've chosen, annoying, but something we can live with. But what's more frustrating after my trek out to the factory between lectures and our nights of colour matching swatches of Colorbond with paint and tile is that the gutters are galvanized instead of the terracotta colour we've ordered.

When Emmanuel suggests we 'just paint them', we're not happy. The idea of taking on yet another job of sealing and double-coating metres of guttering so far above the ground all because of a careless mistake is anathema at this point. When the correct guttering eventually arrives, there's a further delay since they've miscalculated the amount needed and we're four metres short. Meanwhile, the incorrect profile is not taken away despite our requests, but lies for months alongside the driveway of the crowded site until it ends up on top of a skip…yet another instance of the shocking waste that took place on the building sites of not so long ago.

The plasterers are here. Not Emmanuel's usual plastering team who have found work elsewhere, but Don, his son Daniel and a good-looking, well-spoken young man who bonds with the prancing Chihuahuas and whose job it is to keep the plaster coming, and clean the mixer and the barrow afterwards. I've already asked Emmanuel whether he thinks I should mask the window frames and sills with protective tape before the plastering starts, but he's confident that as long as all the timber is properly sealed, it'll be fine. 'I don't think it's necessary,' he says. 'They tend to be pretty careful, these guys.'

And now that the hoist is in place for the roof tiler, the scaffolding can be lowered for the plastering team to start rendering the top half of the outside walls. The plaster will take a week to 'go off' and then we can start the painting while they get on with the inside.

Some months before, we had engaged a colour consultant who had brought a carload of swatches and some preconceived ideas along with her. Although she had plenty of enthusiasm – and she had certainly put in the effort to visit and photograph the raw site before our meeting – she failed to understand the philosophy behind the house: that it incorporated the elements of the Middle East, Spain and Italy, and was therefore suited to colours of warmth and earth. Instead she insisted it must blend with the surrounding houses.

I'm all for blend and synchronicity, but the houses round about are so diverse that our build is but one more piece in an inconsistent puzzle. Consequently, there's nothing to blend with. The recently completed house directly in front is concrete limestone block with a black concrete tile roof; the almost-new one alongside to the north is salmon brick with a grey iron roof; the one in front of that is painted somewhere between watermelon and orange with a cream flat rooftop; and the huge structure to our south is unadulterated Sixties brown brick. But, like the builder's daughter, the consultant was part of the flock she served and she couldn't look beyond her palette of greys and sages with names like sea-mist, mink and moonshine. And each wall, she thought, should be painted a contrasting or complementary colour, the different colours of the facades proclaiming the trend and the edginess of postmodernity.

Richard smiles but he's not really happy.

'This is not quite what we're endeavouring to do here. It's more Mediterranean than anything else.'

She smiles back and she's nice, but it's disappointing. When I had spoken to her earlier, her enthusiasm for our project thrilled down the phone; in practice the passion is certainly there and no doubt the expertise, too, but the empathy, once again with this build that refuses a label, is missing.

It's missing, too, in the 'boutique' paint stores she recommends where you can have any colour you like as long as it shares the spectrum with purples, mauves and greys or olives.

'We were thinking more of a light terracotta or a sort of damaged buff with a hint of apricot…a sort of washed-out colour…'

'Old, old, old. You need to update your thinking a bit.' The salesman fingers the diamond of hair on his chin and gazes out of the window to the traffic building up behind a red light with a faraway look in his eyes.

I try again. 'Do you have anything else, any other colours?'

'They're not selling at the moment. No one wants them. This is our range. Madam. Entire. Anyone who's anyone wants to go this route.

Minimalism, it's called. Clean and bold: colours that suit the houses being built right now. Statements. People are making statements with their houses.' He folds his arms, his gaze still fixed on something I'll never be able to see.

'We're not building that sort of house...' But I've lost him. Or, to be honest, I never really had him. An enormous four wheel drive vehicle pulls up outside the door and as the occupants roll out, his relief is audible. He knows he's onto a hotter prospect than this couple who are determined to go backwards.

We visit other paint stores, all in the slip-slip grip of trend…and end up back at Bunnings with all the choice in the world and now no time to waste. We start by doing a colour test using colour samples to cover huge sheets of plywood. We ask our children to vote. Rest the samples up against the house so they're the first thing we see as we arrive each evening.

In this way we arrive at a colour and in the end we choose Omaha Desert diluted to 50% strength. It's not quite what we're after, but it's not exactly wrong either. Bunnings' price for the many 10-litre tins we need is half what anyone in the 'anyone-whose-anyone' category would pay and we buy bucket-loads of the tried and trusty Dulux that has seen us both – and our homes – through many a successful paint job.

The plasterers have beaten us to the site and Radio 96FM screams out across the river the early morning we front up for this part of our project.

As I'm about to find out, painting the outside of a newly rendered building is a completely different proposition to painting the inside of a house. The actual sealing and painting has its own difficulties, but in addition to this, it's the preparation you have to do in terms of brushing down the render with a stiff-handled broom that makes it so distasteful. It's a filthy job that releases shower after shower of gritty grey sand. A cementy substance that gets into your eyes and ears and settles in the back of your throat. Only after that can you get set to paint.

Now it's been dropped a couple of metres, the scaffolding is easier to climb out onto, but no less dodgy a structure. Our first job is to paint the underside of the boxed-in eaves around the sides and rear of the building and it's actually easier up there on the planks six metres above the ground than it is along the back wall where piles of rubble make it impossible to stand a ladder. As we work backwards around to the front, I see something's up with the rafters we painted a couple of weeks ago. It's not just that they're splattered with grey render: in some places it hangs off like icicles. Later, when I confront Emmanuel, I'm told that it's not the plasterers' job to 'clean up'.

'That's the responsibility of the painters,' he says.

'You mean, they're not going to clean up the mess they've made of the rafters that were only painted a fortnight ago?' I cross my arms. Incredulous and incensed.

'It's the painters' job,' he repeats. 'That stuff. It just wipes off. Who's going to see it up there anyway? Too much fuss and we'll lose them,' he hisses. 'You can't get the trades for love or money right now.'

But I can be stubborn, too. In fact, I'm becoming more stubborn by the nanosecond. I wonder how readily the Turkish painters would have returned to the site to wipe plaster off the painted rafters. Why do I doubt it was built into their quotation?

'This is not fuss, This is going backwards. We've done the job once. And we did a good job.'

Reluctantly, he agrees to talk to them. When, a few days later, nothing has happened, I ask them myself and the young boy who for most part lolls about talking to the dogs swings up onto the scaffolding with a rag in his hand and wipes most of it off.

The scaffolding had its difficulties – there wasn't a time I stepped out onto the mismatched boards that I didn't have to give myself a pep talk – but it was nothing compared to the day we're faced with the immensity of the lower half of the north face of the building. About an hour into the job, the day is starting to heat up, my arms and shoulders to ache and, despite my cotton gloves, my hands beginning to blister. The extender rod my roller is attached to is lighter than Richard's, but it's also shorter, which means I have to stretch every ligament in my body to reach the spot where the trim around the house is eventually going to cover evidence of the join between the top and bottom halves of the building. And, even though we've given the wall a thorough brushing, as the roller parts with its paint it still tends to collect small grains of cement-sand until it's as heavy as a lump of concrete. With each sweep up and down the tall wall, I'm grunting like Venus Williams in the U.S. Open and my neck is starting to make clicking sounds at being held at such an impossible angle.

'I can't do this,' I say to Richard and it somehow helps to verbalise the impossibility of this latest task we've set ourselves.

Because there's no way back. Each wall gets three coats in all: first, the oil-based tinted sealer which we allow to dry for more than a day and then two coats of Omaha and, like everything I've ever attempted, I have to admit it does get easier. I learn to load the roller thoroughly and evenly with paint before rolling it well along the ribs of the tray. An even distribution of paint on the roller translates to a smooth layer of paint on the wall. To avoid an unsightly 'joining' line, you need to paint from top to bottom in one go instead of painting the high bit with the extension and then unscrewing the roller to work more easily on the bottom layer. Professional painters stand well back, start the loaded roller in the middle of the wall, roll an M or a W from top to bottom and then fill in the gaps. Each day I learn something new.

Meanwhile the plasterers are working on the inside walls where again we find plaster splashed and splattered over the wooden frames and sills. I pray they'll sponge it off at the end of the day before it sets.

As they wash up and prepare to leave, I ask the bossman's son Daniel, 'You're not going to leave them like that? Surely? These sills are wood. They'll spoil. Do you think you could hose it off?'

Carefully picking flecks of plaster off his nose, he regards me for a moment. Shrugs. 'Can't put water anywhere near it for a week.'

I insist Emmanuel meet me on site.

'You told me it wasn't necessary to cover these sills…now just look at this. All that wood…' My voice wobbles when I think of the afternoons and evenings of sanding and sealing. I look at the timber bubbling grey.

'Ach. Easy to fix, comes off easily.' Before I know what he's about, he slips a screwdriver out of his pocket and digs it into the sill to loosen the plaster. And all at once I know this is a man who doesn't understand wood.

'No, no,' I plead. I think my hand rests on his sleeve. 'Just leave it.' As the screwdriver digs again, my lids are pricking. 'Please…please just… leave it. Leave it alone.' I leave him with Richard.

Outside a ute has navigated the other parked cars to unload its consignment of glass. A young fellow with laugh lines white against the tan of his face stops in his task of unloading a stash of glass.

'What's up? You seem upset.' Gently he sets down a heavy pane.

'Oh, nothing really. Well, actually, it *is* something. In there.' I nod up the concrete stairway. 'It's all that wood – the windows and doors – being ruined with splashed plaster. I can't believe it…'

He passes the thick leather of his gloves briefly across his face, pushes back his hat.

'Look. Really. It's nothing to get upset about. Has the stuff been sealed?'

I nod. 'Oil. But only oil.'

'Good enough. Then the plaster'll wipe off. Really it will. I used to work on houses up in Queensland…North Queensland. There's a lot of timber up there and this happens all the time. It actually wipes off quite easily with a wet cloth. Then you'll want to apply Sikkens Supernatural. Don't forget that. "Supernatural" it's called. Two, maybe three, coats. Any plaster marks on the wood will just disappear and you won't have to re-do the job for about 10 years. That's been my experience. Cheer up. It'll come good. You'll see.'

He has the sort of smile that vibrates through his whole body and I feel better instantly. Out of nowhere I find myself hoping he has a girlfriend who knows he's very special.

Meanwhile, Rolf is getting towards the end of the brickwork and one of his final jobs on this site is to build the curved wall of the staircase. We'd discussed this at some length with Emmanuel at the beginning of the job and had been invited to view an example that winds up through several floors in his own very smart townhouse.

'All I did…' he had said at that time, taking a pencil out of his top pocket and attaching an imaginary string, '…was tie a string to the end of a pencil, like so, anchor the end of the string where I wanted it and pivot the pencil around like this…like a compass. See?'

The wall of Emmanuel's staircase was a perfect arc, very similar to the magazine version we had shown him, similar, too, to the original inspiration back at Girton College in Cambridge. But in Rolf's version, this wall is angular, nothing like the elegant curve I had envisioned. In the end, he builds that wall three times…until, finally, it's closer to what we had in mind. Later I find the original magazine photograph screwed up on top of one of the heaps of rubble.

Our consignment of marble arrives: five crates in all that each weigh one tonne and have to be hoisted to one side of the site by a Hiab.

'Who are you going to get to lay the marble?' Emmanuel asks one day.

'We are.'

'You? You are going to lay that marble? All those tiles?' He looks at me as if I'm tucking into a meal of roast beef during an outbreak of mad cow.

'Yes.'

'It's not possible.' He shakes his head. 'You can't do that. Have you any idea how specialized a job it is to lay marble? You can't be a millimetre out. It's precise, a precision job. They're not forgiving like other tiles: the screed has to be perfect, like a mirror, even a grain of sand can throw you out. Believe me, I know. My brother's a tiler and together we laid some the finest marble in the world…Carrera Italian marble. But it was one of the most difficult jobs…'

'This is a little more rustic than Carrera, so it's probably less important to have it mirror flat. Really, we can handle it…'

'I'll find a marble tiler. I think I know someone I can get. The wet rooms are already in the contract. After that you can decide if you want him to do the rest of the house.'

He's adamant and we agree that the tiler will do the bathrooms and, if he does a good job, we can negotiate with him for the remainder. But it's during this conversation it comes up that the arcades are also to be marble. Emmanuel scratches his head.

'Marble? But there's no screed there. There's no slab laid in the arcades. I thought you were going to brick those pathways.'

'Brick? No, never brick. That would track too much grit into the house. But we did wonder why you didn't pour the slab for arcades at the same time as the rest. We thought you were going to do it when you did the garage floor and the back steps.'

'But they – these pathways – were going to be brick.'

We're going round in circles.

'No,' I repeat, 'never brick. They were always meant to be an extension of the living areas just like the front balcony. They're on the plan under the main roof. They've been an integral part of the house since we signed up.'

We're both angry. It's obvious that assumptions have been made on both our parts and we're both incorrect. Emmanuel measures up and that's yet another variation to our monthly bill.

The floor tiler is Yugoslavian, newly arrived in the country, and looks like some sort of blond god. The first night he comes to introduce himself, his wife comes along too. And I can't say I blame her. I think if I were her I'd bring his smoko snacks and his lunchpack to the site, too. Every hour.

It makes me wonder – not for the first time – where the tradeswomen are. I hear tell they exist, but certainly there are none on this site or any other building site I've visited. The Australian building industry is screaming out for tradespeople, and, at the same time, there are women looking for a job in the open air. I find it incredible that women in today's world still overlook training in one of the many building trades. And how about those women you hear on talkback radio complaining how difficult it is to meet a man? Well, here they are, the men – all types, like any cross section of the community – with some real charmers among them. It beats going to a bar to meet a man. And the competition is nowhere to be seen.

'Anything,' this man states shyly in answer to my question as to whether laying marble presents any difficulties. 'I can do all tile: marble, all.'

But evidently it's not part of his job description to carry the tiles from the ground to the main floor. That's our job. They're heavy: the most I can lug at any one time is four, Richard six. And they're sharp: that's the rectified edge we were after, I remind myself.

The tiler insists on wider grout than we'd planned. Goggled and covered in marble dust, his long fine fingers ungloved as he pushes the tiles towards the busy blade of the angle grinder, he looks just as godlike as he did in the driveway. But we wanted as fine a grout as possible, as grout tends to be the main upkeep problem with a tiled floor, so I persist.

'We were hoping to get away with minimum of grouting: preferably none at all.'

'No!' He's horrified, looks up for a moment, his fingers inches from the whirring blade. 'You *must* have grout.' Takes me into the bathroom to explain the cunning of water, how it can find its way through a hair's crack. 'Through the smallest fraction of a millimetre. Like this.' He holds up his hand with thumb and forefinger almost touching. 'It can also reappear a long way from where it enters. And then, I tell you, you have trouble. Big trouble. Believe me, I know what I'm talking about.'

He does a good job, but he finds the variations in the thickness of the Indonesian marble tiles a challenge. The scream of the grinder and the unrelenting dust convince me surprisingly easily that Emmanuel is right about the difficulty and magnitude of this job. I ask the tiler for a quote for the rest of the house and I'm not surprised when he says he's too busy. He has jobs lined up and all of them closer to home than this one, he says. And so, for the moment, we leave it there. With the long-awaited moving-in date coming up fast, perhaps we'll just have to get the rooms tiled one by one after we move in.

When he leaves the site for the last time, he takes his grinder with him, but leaves the rest of his tools lying in a heap. I contact the builder.

'Means nothing,' he says. 'Have you any idea how much these tradesmen are earning at the moment? The tools are nothing.'

The end of another illusion: that their tools are sacred to tradesmen.

We've worked hard to keep up with the plasterers when suddenly they aren't there anymore. No Emmanuel, no Rolf, no plasterers and, according to the builder's office, the electrician's been held up because it's his grandmother's funeral. Without 96FM at full tilt the house is quiet and lonely-looking, a ghost build rearing up out of its bed of dusty debris.

We have plenty to do ourselves, but it's demoralizing to see everything stop once again. A slab was laid for a house down the road just a few months ago and already it's up, roofed and rendered.

But the timing is good to build the last of the limestone boundary walls while the site is deserted. I leave a message for Dave on his mobile and he rings me back three days later.

'Sorry, missed your call. My grandmother died over East and we had to go to the funeral.' When he turns up, he's unusually morose, so much so I'm moved to say how sorry I am, although I must admit there's a cynical part of me – a hangover from the excuses attached to student essays handed in late – that questions the coincidental deaths of two grandmothers on one site within a couple of days. But he nods and hangs his head in such a way I'm forced to doubt my own doubts. Besides, there was that whole issue with the moving of the rubbish, so I'm not exactly on the front foot here.

I can't sleep again, and I'm on site before the sun comes up. For the first time, I use a new ladder with a platform. It has a railing in front which works not only as a safety device, but is also useful for hanging a paint tin or water flask. If I need to use the roller, the platform is just wide enough for me to stand with a paint tray sandwiched between my feet. In fact, I'd be set for an hour at a time if only I didn't have to climb down every five or ten minutes to move the ladder. I'm about to start work on the study ceiling while wondering how long it will be before someone invents an e-ladder with its own motor when I see a ute turn off the road and the plasterers rattle up the driveway with trailer and mixer in tow. It's been well over a week since they were on site. Another grandmother?

'We missed you,' I say as Daniel's head appears above the stairs.

'Birthday party.' He touches a match to the end of a cigarette and leans back against Rolf's staircase wall.

'Gracious. It must have been some party. For more than a week, ten days?' I dip the roller into the paint.

'Melbourne. We went to Melbourne.'

'Melbourne…for a birthday party?'

He shrugs, draws deeply on his smoke and blows circles up the ladder steps as he watches me roll the paint. His stare is intense. I can feel this more than I can see it.

'How long is it we have to wait before we can paint the inside walls?' I keep my eyes fixed on the roller moving back and forth across the ceiling.

'Better give it time.' Obviously not a talkative man.

'Yes, but how much time? As long as we waited for the outside? Should we give it a week, for instance?'

'More. Longer than that.'

I start to burn under his gaze. If there were more women in the trades, one wouldn't be such an anomaly. Wonder whether my jeans are too tight. Ceilings are hell on the neck.

'Two weeks then? Three? Four?' I'm fed up with the quiz show.

'More. Say, six. Minimum.'

'Six weeks! Why so long?' The roller sags in my hand, drips. I look down at him lolling against the wall. 'That's ages.'

He shrugs again, flings the cigarette butt on the floor, grinds it into the screed. 'That's what it takes. You don't want the plaster to fall off the walls, like.'

I wonder at the house that's shot up down the road. Bet they didn't wait six weeks before starting to paint. And the project homes that are built with the owners in residence within three months. I'm darned sure they don't wait six weeks either. But when I query it with Emmanuel, he agrees that's what it takes for plaster to cure.

When the builder's electrician finally shows up, we run through the crosses we've transposed from the house plan to their appropriate places on the walls. Everything goes smoothly until he refuses to install power points in two of the bathrooms.

'No, I can't do that until the shower screens are in place.'

'We're not having shower screens upstairs. Only downstairs.'

'No shower screens?' He's incredulous. But we don't want shower cubicles. We've been through all this a number of times already with the draftsman, the builder and the tiler. I explain all this carefully. He draws his tape from his pocket, but doesn't use it. Just stands there holding it in the palm of his hand. 'In that case, no power points. Definitely. It's illegal. I'll lose my licence.' With a shake of his head, he slips the tape back in his pocket, moves towards the door.

'I'm not suggesting you do anything illegal. We don't want to do anything illegal either…obviously. Just put the outlets anywhere in the room you're allowed to. How about on the opposite wall over there?'

'No,' he shakes his head. More vehemently than before. 'I won't do it. It's not worth my licence.'

'But it'll be further away from the water than the one in my bathroom. Why is it all right there and not here? I'm just trying to understand the logic, that's all.'

But he's completely unnerved by the idea of showers without screens; his mind is in a loop that keeps returning him to the same point, and I drop the request for the time being and we move on with the rest of the job.

Later, Emmanuel calls me and demands we put in screens.

'Everyone has them,' he insists.

'We never intended to put in screens. They're not on the plan. And how is it compulsory so long as it's not transgressing the safety laws and regulations? I can show you a dozen magazine pictures where…' But he's fed up with me and my magazine pictures.

'Phuf…magazines,' he says. 'You can't believe them. Take my word for it. Anyway my electrician is not coming back to sign off on the job until you get screens. That means the whole job will be held up.'

We're ready for the last of the bricking jobs: the front steps and a set of steps up to what will be the vegetable garden at the rear of the block, but Rolf's away because one of his family is unwell. So a substitute brickie arrives, gets halfway through building the set of three steps before he hits his thumb with the hammer. He goes off to get it fixed, leaves the job incomplete and his tools sitting in the rubble. We never see him again.

Meanwhile I speak to an electrician friend of ours and explain the shower screen stand-off.

'He's absolutely right if the point is within a certain distance of the shower. I'll come round and have a look. I want to have a look at that build of yours anyway.'

When he arrives, for once Emmanuel is on site. Although I introduce our friend merely as a friend, there's something in the look the two give each other that reminds me of the situation with the roof tiler all over again.

Once we're in the problem bathroom, our friend measures the distance between where the power point had been marked on the plan – and thus the wall – and the water source.

'He's right. You can't have it there, too close. But how about on the opposite wall? Wouldn't that be more convenient for a power point anyway?'

'Yes, near the basin. Hmm, much better. That's what I thought, too.' I shake my head. 'But he won't do it.'

'Just tell him to put a regular power switch there then. Later you can get someone to change it over for you. Totally within the legal requirements. But I must say,' he adds, 'in terms of the getting the house finished I thought you'd be a lot further on than this.'

'An amazing number of grandmothers seem to be passing on. I don't know whether it's a coincidence. Or the heat.'

'Grandmothers?' He laughs. 'Come to think of it, I've used that one myself a few times…'

At this point, we're fast coming towards the end of the third year of the lease we'd originally taken out for nine months. Along with Richard's fulltime workday and my own work that currently involves my lecturing and tutoring commitments and finishing off what painting I can fit in, a typical list of a day's phone calls follows:
+ Call Prestige (limestone garden walls)
+ Call Handcarved Stone (Indonesian marble)
+ Call granite company (kitchen countertop)
+ Call lattice (for down the boundary alongside the Spanish steps to mitigate the effects of the crooked boundary erected by our politician neighbour)
+ Call re the lift (we still have a hole where the lift is to go)

- Call Pilkington's (glass for owner-supplied windows and bifold doors)
- Call carpenter (to fit the literally thousands of strips of beading around the window frames)
- Call plumber
- Call Allwest (louvre windows in the bedroom, also owner-supplied)
- Call John (wrought iron balustrade for balcony)

Regarding this last dot-point, over time, we've had a number of different ideas for the balcony balustrade. The City R-Codes call for a metre-high wall or railing. We don't want total railing because of the complicated aesthetics involved in seeing chair, table and human legs, trousers and/ or skirts through the bars, but we don't want the blankness of a solid wall either. We like the idea of decorative brick, but see a sample only by chance in a tiling shop where it's not for sale. It's available overseas, but not here. For a time, we toy with the idea of bringing the bricks in, but for the relatively small quantity we need it's not a realistic proposition.

In the end, we decide the wrought iron railing in the townhouse is one of the more attractive features of our rental and I source the name of a wrought iron craftsman. We meet with John and Nancy in their new home over a cup of brewed coffee and home-baked cookies and they relate their own horror stories of the recent build.

'But we're still here to tell the tale,' he says getting off his stool. 'Come to my workshop.'

'But not before you had a heart attack over it all,' his wife calls after him, and it makes me wonder, not for the first time, what it is about these house builds that causes so much stress, because stress it certainly is.

And if what we are going through appears to you as one long list of difficulties one after another, that's what building in boom times was for us. A word that my daughter Tammy used after the birth of her first child comes to mind. She described the feed/change/feed cycle of the baby's early weeks as 'relentless'. And that's the best way to explain this sequence of events in which we're well and truly ensnarled. Whether you label the individual issues that present themselves as challenges, problems, or difficulties – or whitewash them as 'opportunities for growth' or the wearing of coloured hats – one thing's for sure: they're certainly relentless. And where, taken separately, with a bit of space in between and less emotional attachment, you could relegate them to an 'all in a day's work' cliché, it's the cumulative effect that wears you down.

Because lying like a film of sticky dust over these smaller comparatively insignificant issues is the larger picture. For one thing, there's the money invested in the project which, for most of us in the Western world, is the biggest outlay and commitment we're likely to make in a lifetime. For another, it returns us once again to one of the most primal needs of all: shelter. From there it's a short step to boundaries and guarding our own territory. I suspect this is why we are so quick to spring to the defence of our homes. And why even the most unassuming property can attain the dimensions of a mansion in the eyes of its owners. Certainly, the movie *The Castle* was ostensibly about the Aussie qualities of mateship and fair go, but as its name suggests, at its core, it was something more than that, too. It was about pride in a home and the size or grandeur of that home was never an issue.

The cottage in North Fremantle was my castle. It didn't matter that for a long while after I moved in, the toilet chain was a piece of fraying rope and that the floor sloped like the wrecked deck of the *Mary Deare*. With paint, plaster and a fair dollop of patience it came together; by the time I had my rugs out on the polished floors, my bits of brass and copper strategically placed, my father's portrait hanging grandly in the lounge, the house was a home, yes, but something more than that, too. Many an evening after my late-night walk along the river with the Ridgeback brothers I'd come home to linger outside the lounge window. I was drawn by the softness of a glow so golden it never failed to spark a sense of wonder at how this had been achieved with ordinary globes, cheap shades and persistence. I have no talent in interior design – and at that time not a spare cent to help it along – but in spite of me, what a rich tableau had come together. And what pleasure it provided during a period when pleasures were few and far between, those moments of voyeurism into my own life.

I shake my mind free of the past and bring it back to the here and now in John's workshop where Richard is being treated to the technicalities of bending iron. It's clear, even without paying proper attention to what the men have been saying, that once again we've lucked out in finding someone who has enormous pride in his work. This is evident without hearing the words. It's tucked away in the information garnered from the lightness in the touch of his fingers as he slides them along the curves of the iron bars. Just as there are those who love working with wood, here is not only someone who loves metal, but who is also one of that fast-fading breed of master craftsmen.

Richard has made a pattern for the balcony that duplicates the ironwork scrolls on the top segment of our gates and it is this that John copies as he fashions the lengths of iron to be set onto the part-wall of the balcony in the gaps between each of the five pillars.

By now, we have almost finished painting the outside of the house and are well on our way to completing the painting of the ceilings before the electrician installs the halogen lights.

My next job will be to paint the cornices. We've specified the larger Oxford profile throughout the house: deep, angular, multi-layered cornices designed to complement the three-metre-high ceilings and contrast with the curves of the building. Instead, an entire consignment of the smaller version is delivered and once again there is a delay as we wait for our specified order.

Emmanuel can't see why we can't use the smaller version. In fact, he thinks the larger Oxford will look clumsy and out of place. He makes a good case, but we're just as adamant that the smaller profile will look mean and skimpy at the top of the high walls. When the correct ones are finally delivered, we get only half the quantity at first as the factory races to keep up with demand, but as they go up, they look good and we know we've got it right.

The only time I doubt our choice in this regard is in the painting of these multi-stepped lengths of plaster. When a professional painter quotes on a paint job for a new building, does he check out such detail as cornicing? Because the ones we've chosen have ten surfaces and each surface has to be individually brushed. That means that for every couple of metres of cornice, which is the extent of my reach before I have to get down to move the ladder, there are ten separate surfaces to brush. In all, I circle each room three times as each surface has three coats, and more in some cases where the plaster is too factory-fresh. If I thought painting the broad expanse of the north face of the building was tedious, this is mind-numbingly worse. To begin with, I occupy my mind by working out just how many metres lie ahead; when this gets too depressing, I start to sing and when this becomes too limiting, I begin to compose my songs as I go along. At that time, I didn't know to what extent sound travels near water. Now I know that in this area it probably reaches across the river. And into the neighbours' kitchens, too. Surprising, really, that anyone talks to us at all by the time we move in. But in this way, many metres of cornice are covered with paint.

And so are we when Karen and Alex turn up with cups of strong coffee one evening. Too tired to care what we look like, we perch where we can amid the broken brick and tile at the foot of the huge building that's bit by bit taking shape, and as I suck in the bitter drink, I know that this is what makes friendship. This arriving unannounced with cups of coffee strongly laced with thoughtfulness. 'It's the journey, not the arrival that matters,' wrote Leonard Woolf, Virginia's husband. And what a journey this is turning out to be.

We walk past this empty block with its nine-metre drop for over a year before we fall for its challenge.

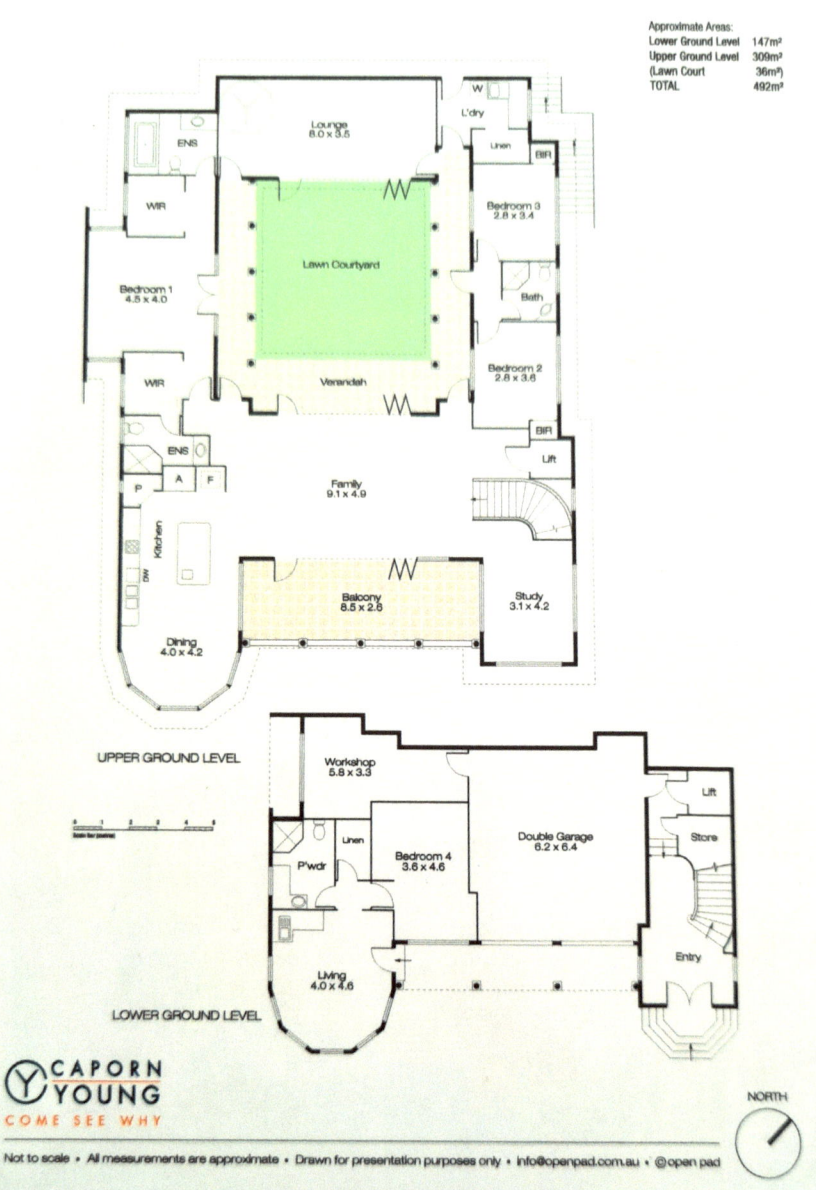

The final floor plan was somewhat different from our earlier intentions.
Photo by kind permission of Director Steve Currie of Caporn Young

The first bricks. We're on our way as the retaining walls go up on the lower part of the block.

The house is slowly taking shape.

Richard's energy is amazing.

Despite the owners' doubts, the view is everything we could want in a 16ft...

But will the courtyard eventually fulfil our rather high expectations? At this point, we wonder.

Very little space to move on the crowded block.

Our two little rescue Chihuahuas – Miggie and Zorro – playing on the unfinished balcony one early morning.

THE DARKEST NIGHT

But every journey finally draws to an end, and for us the date of the elusive 'lock-up' is fast approaching. In discussion with Emmanuel, we set the date for December 19 and look forward to spending Christmas in our new home.

But it's not until I've finished the last of the Curriculum Council's TEE English Literature marking that the realisation really hits me that we're finally able to give up the lease on the townhouse. I remember how we'd initially tossed up as to whether we should rent for six months or nine and how we'd decided to 'camp' for the few months when we first moved in. Now, almost three years later, we are more than half unpacked, but it's still felt a lot like camping. Nevertheless the rental has done us well and has been convenient in every respect, and also – not a small thing – we've been very lucky to be able to extend the lease five times. We know people who've had to move several times while their homes were being built and the idea of that on top of everything else doesn't bear thinking about.

But it's also been a period of feeling a bit like a fish on the dry edge of a pond with the water temptingly close but out of reach. Now it's over. I've booked two large trucks for Monday and cancelled the rental lease as from the end of the following week. All that remains to be done is to carefully re-seal what we can, and pack and label the boxes we'll need for the first few months in the new house.

The new house. Strange to call it that. It doesn't look very new really. Just hopelessly incomplete, a mess to be honest, with most of its inside walls unpainted and dusty screed floors. But the doors and windows are in and the electrics close to being completed and if we don't move before the builder's break, we're stymied. It'll be well into February before everything starts to wind up again.

I feel strangely light and happy. After these long years of constant decision making, the only decision facing us at the moment is whether we move into the flat downstairs while we complete the upper storey or vice versa. Both areas have the same lack of paint and tile and so it doesn't much matter which way we do it.

Once again it's late afternoon on the Friday before the scheduled Monday move when a fax comes through. I scan it quickly and then, as it gets my attention, I read it again word by galling word. It's not Friday 13th, but it might just as well be from the tone and content of the letter.

"Following a site visit today we wish to advise that we cannot recommend handover of your property as it has by no means reached the level of practical completion required for such to take place…" A list of eight items follows that still have to be completed, the first two – glazing and the supply of door hardware – are By Owner, the others By Builder. As Emmanuel well knows, there's no hold-up from our end. We've had the hardware for the doors in hand for a week waiting for his carpenter to turn up; the 'glazing' refers to two of the bifolds which are only external in that they both open up onto the courtyard which is internal to the building.

But right now it doesn't matter because the long and short of it is that Emmanuel is not prepared to hand over the site. I perch on one of the recently repacked cartons, force myself to concentrate. The chemical smell of the fax paper makes my eyes smart. This means we're not able to move. This means I have to cancel the movers' trucks. This means we'll have to spend Christmas here. This may mean we'll have to spend Christmas somewhere else entirely if this place has already been re-let. It also may mean we have to sit out the builder's break until the end of February. Another two months. I rest the letter on my knee and gaze up the long passage piled with boxes waiting to be sealed. I wonder whether this whole project has got to me, whether there's some mistake, whether

I'm reading things right. My mouth is dry. I can hear the dogs snoring in the back room. A car passing by on the road outside.

But no, it's true. We can't move. The builder deems the house not yet at lock-up. If we go ahead and move anyway, an action he strongly advises against, we will not be insured.

The piece of fax paper rattling in my hands is the only thing that's got body. I don't know how to tell Richard, so I call my daughter first and her clear commiseration returns the feeling to my legs.

I'm so angry because it's so unexpected. It's really eleventh-hour stuff and, quite apart from my own disappointment, unless they can slot in another job, the family-run removal company is going to be left with two large trucks empty for a full day the week before Christmas.

I light another stick of incense and place it in the Buddha's hands, watch as the smoke spirals around my frustration and hot ash burns yet another hole in the balsa wood balcony.

Stalling still before I have the courage to tell Richard, I call my father. 'Ah,' he says. 'The darkest night heralds the brightest dawn, darling. Always does. It's a bonanza, that house. It'll all work out, you'll see.'

I phone the trucking company next and then the leasing agents. There's a tense few moments as they check if the townhouse is still available, but there's still someone looking after us. How lucky are we to be able to extend the lease yet again.

When I finally read my husband the letter over the phone, I only know he's still the other end of the line because I can hear his breathing.

'That's all he says?'

'Yes, that's all.'

'Well, there's nothing we can do about it then, is there,' he says in a voice that sounds like it's been rolled between two sheets of baking paper.

When I go to bed that night I practise my *Let go, let God* mantra. I am so weary of pushing this bonanza of a build uphill.

And then there's the hand again that reaches for mine and he holds me tight through the howling of the dogs in the pound until we go to sleep.

And if I need proof things happen for a reason, in retrospect it becomes clear that the delay is, once again, not all bad.

Having sorted and moved every piece of the five tonnes of Indonesian marble from where it was stacked by the Hiab to a less intrusive spot on the cramped site, we realize we might now have time to get at least some of the floors tiled before we move in. We decide to use the time we have available to at least get the living area and our bedroom suite tiled. After leaving many messages for tradesmen who don't call back, I return from university one day to find a message from a firm of commercial floor tilers headed by two Spanish brothers.

What is it about tilers? Where the bathroom tiler was an Adonis, Gabriel, the Spanish team leader with his flashing dark brown eyes, makes Antonio Banderas look like the boy next door. But more importantly his prices are competitive, his firm's testimonials outstanding and he's used to working on large projects. Over the past week, the only other floor tiler game enough to return my call quailed at the scale of the job, yet another reminder – if I need one – that there's so much work around, the trades are in the happy position of being able to pick and choose.

Everything's suddenly easy. We sign a contract with the Spaniards that covers the tiling of the flat downstairs, the living area upstairs and our bedroom suite. The arcades and the rest of the house can wait. Gabriel comes to look at the job, inspects the tiles, and estimates his team will complete it in five or six working days. This job is perfect for him, he says – a filler between two shopping centre projects – and he'll start the following week.

It's a clear and beautiful January morning the day they're due to start. The sun burns its way through the bright haze over the river to turn the water shimmery with gold and silver sprinkles. It's a day to sing. How lucky we've been able to extend our lease and how particularly fortunate to be able to move in with tiled floors. Things happen for a reason. As I get out of the car the air is fresh and feisty with effervescence or expectation or both.

But there's no response to my cheery good morning and, when I reach the top of the stairs, not very much happening. In fact, work-wise, it would be perfectly accurate to say *nothing* is happening.

A group of eight marble tiles is laid out neatly in the middle of the floor. Gabriel is striding back and forth with a mobile phone pressed tight to his ear and four or five men are standing about fidgeting and waiting like extras on a film set. One has found something that captures his attention several kilometres away, another traces circles in the cement dust with his foot. Another just hangs his head, arms crossed. When their boss finally flicks off his phone and drops it in his top pocket, he gets straight to the point.

'We can't lay these.' Hands on hips, Gabriel nods his head at the group of tiles.

'You can't?'

'Won't.'

'Oh. Why not?'

'These tiles. See. They're all over the place. Badly cut. The dimensions of each tile are different. Look.' He pokes the toe of his shoe at one of the tiles on the floor in front of him.

'But we went through this. You saw the tiles. We discussed the different thicknesses and you said…you said you would take care of that in the grouting process…'

'Huh. Different thicknesses are nothing. That we can handle. No problem. The difficulty here is that these tiles are all different *sizes*. Some are not even straight.' He squats down, taps a tile. 'See? See here. Not much, but it doesn't take much once you start multiplying the error. In a large space like this, by the time we reach the end of the room, the line will be crooked, way out…'

'The bathrooms have worked well…'

'Small areas like that, yes, I agree, not so bad.' He lays one tile on top of another.

It's true: now he's pointing it out, I can see there's a difference in size, and it's not just thickness. I feel myself heating up as I remember Emmanuel's words about the exactitude of marble laying.

'I don't have time to have my men measuring each tile…' he continues.

'If there's a problem – Richard and I – we'll measure them. We can do that. We can check them.' My words reflect back at me, sounding desperate. I want to add 'please', but I'm begging as it is. The team has given up all pretense of finding something more interesting outside the room and we have their full attention.

Gabriel's eyes meet mine and they're not flashing now; in fact they're quite flat and hard as he says, 'I refuse to have my men lay them. These tiles will not make a good job. But as a compromise…as a compromise we'll do downstairs. I'll leave one of my men here and he can complete that in two, say three, days.' His phone rings and he digs it out, glances at the message, flicks it off impatiently.

'And if you can get new tiles…get Italian. Preferably a larger size than these – 400mm x 400mm work best – then we can start on this top area next Monday. I'll give my men a holiday until then.'

I try to collect myself, think of the five tonnes of marble sitting in the crates at the edge of the block. 'But all these tiles we have already…' I'm not exactly wailing or wringing my hands, but I'm aware the pitch of my voice is unusually high and Edward de Bono's hats are far from my thoughts right now.

'Not my problem.' His voice is crisp. His phone rings again and he swings away. The show is over and his men move slowly to pick up their things.

My mind is racing. When I think of the dozens of tiling shops we visited, the samples we deliberated on, our search for the elusive marble that came from the Red Mountain, our delight when we placed the red and cream side by side and the time it all took to make a final decision I wonder how on earth we can choose another tile for delivery before the following Monday. Not only that, but it's yet more expense. Italian tiles will be double what we paid for these.

'What are we going to do?' I'm almost crying when I call Richard, but he's as cool as always. We go over our options and discuss moving into the flat downstairs and waiting to get the main floor tiled until the trades are less busy. Or doing it ourselves as we had originally planned.

'Why don't you get on to Monica at Bernini's,' he says at last. 'She was very obliging in our choice of marble offcuts for the vanities in the bathrooms. See what she has to offer.'

Bernini is probably one of Perth's most popular marble importers and Monica had been very helpful in digging out a leftover slab of French onyx for my bathroom vanity. I call her straight away.

'Monica, it's Tangea. We're in trouble. Help.'

'Come straight over,' she says when I finish. 'I'll see what I can do. If you can tell me how many you need, I'll see whether we have them in stock. We do keep small quantities of some of the marbles. Or travertine. Come to think of it, from the way you describe your house, travertine might even suit you better. And it's cheaper.'

I sit in her office as she flicks through screen after screen of factory stock. In the end, there are two or three possibilities, all nearly double the price of the Indonesian marble.

Later that morning I drive out to the industrial area where the Bernini factory is situated, wander around the huge hangar while a forklift driver lifts sample after sample from the high shelves to the floor and kindly lays them out for me.

'One tile is no good…you need to see as many as possible together to have any idea at all what the floor will look like.'

In the end, it comes down to a shortlist of three travertine tiles. I take back samples to set out in the garden of the townhouse for Richard to make his choice that lunchtime. We both like Santa Barbara, a honed light buff, 400mm-square travertine tile we think will blend well enough

THE DARKEST NIGHT

with the bathroom tiles we already have in place and which will achieve the particular combination of warmth and classic elegance we're after. They're able to deliver by Friday. Happily, I call Gabriel to tell him the problem is solved, call Monica to thank her for her quick work, leave a message for Handcarved Stone to tell them that the tiles are not square, the tilers refuse to lay them and to ask whether they are prepared to take half the consignment back.

And then I slowly blow out the breath I've been holding since ten o'clock this morning and make myself a cup of tea.

It's at this point I receive an email from my friend Anne. She had been my best friend for the three years we spent together at Msongari Convent in Nairobi. At thirteen we'd invented all sorts of things together, our mythical racehorses – my Crown Jewel and her Beau Vite – and laid out our plans for our later lives. Our husbands would be tall and handsome and, above all, faithful. We'd have mansions, both of us. She'd have six children; I wanted only two. And the dogs, horses, gardens and parties we would have. All very grand and minutely detailed. Written out on sheets of thick bond paper which for some reason had ended up in my possession and which I'd tucked into the corners of suitcases and boxes and saved over move after move around the world in the forty-odd years since then.

I mean to tell her I've kept our visions intact, long after things have not happened for either of us in quite the way we'd imagined they would. I sort of think that maybe we'll have a cup of tea together one day, hold the dreams for a moment longer and then put them to rest with the reverence they deserve and the realism that is.

Some time before we'd left Lockhart Street, I'd contacted her to say we were coming to England and that I'd love to catch up. It was an opportunity to meet some thirty years after the trip we took to Thailand when we were both nineteen years old. The trip was memorable for many reasons, but I'll never forget the train journey from Kuala Lumpur to Bangkok when she'd held onto my belt as we both balanced on the couplings between carriages while I vomited my guts out over the rail tracks whizzing darkly underneath.

To my ebullient and enthusiastic email, she'd replied somewhat hesitantly.

'Come? To visit? Well yes…of course you must come.' And I took it that perhaps it wasn't frightfully convenient. Or that she didn't want me to come. Or whatever you think in those circumstances. Anyway, I was sort of childishly hurt she wasn't thrilled.

So I left it that time, we went to the UK, and in the rather haphazard way of our communication, it must be nearly four years since we last corresponded.

"Please write," she emails now. "Write everything. Write everything about your life."

So even though everything isn't too flash right now given the stasis we're in, I sit down immediately to tell her everything. Pages and pages. The good and the bad. Zap it on its way.

A couple of days later a reply wings back on the new computer my son Viv has set up for me. From her husband Nick.

'I'm sad to have to tell you that Anne has passed away. She had cancer of the colon, then metastasis. She fought bravely, but she died.'

You see, says my mother from another realm. Never let the sun go down on your anger. Or you'll be the one that suffers.

It wasn't anger, but it amounted to the same thing in the end, didn't it? Because tangled up with the grief there is another layer, a coating of deep regret. Regret we didn't have that cup of tea together. Regret we couldn't giggle over our rotten attempts at forecasting the future. Regret that we didn't get a chance to show our beautiful children to each other. Regret I didn't know she was sick until it was too late. Regret I'll not see her again this side of the Great Divide. Regret that I just didn't call in on her regardless.

Regrets, I've had my share…

Gabriel's tiler does such a good job on the flat downstairs with the Indonesian tiles I can't help wondering what the fuss was about. With the tall 3.5 metre ceilings we have on the ground floor, the tiled rooms look cool and airy, the walls now ready for their creamy coatings of Dulux Stone Pillar.

I'm wondering how far they've got with the main floor as I run up the stairs at lunchtime the following Monday. There's a team of two men today working in the far corner and Gabriel with his phone to his ear as usual. He smiles when he sees me, clicks off.

'Beautiful tiles. You've made the right choice. My favourites. I've done a big shopping centre with these. Just recently. They look beautiful down. You won't regret it.'

I glow under the praise.

'But there's another problem,' he says, kicking at a wave in the cement of the slab, an action that echoes somewhere in the middle of my stomach. 'This is terrible screed. I'm not sure how we're going to handle this.' He points to a beam lying horizontally across the main floor. 'Look. If I go to one end…and step on it like this, the other end lifts off by about five centimeters, maybe more. Do you see? This floor has a high spot in the centre. If I tile it like this, I can't guarantee the tiles won't crack. And, if you have a big table, for example, it will wobble about. See…here.'

I see all right: the beam balances like a seesaw.

'But the adhesive,' I say. 'Or the grout. Surely you can make the adhesive thicker and that will take care of the difference?'

'That much?' His laugh is sour.

'How about building it all up right through to the verandah wall?'

'We can't do that,' he points out. 'The tracking for the folding doors is already in place.'

'Let me call Emmanuel to see if he has any ideas.' I'm angry. Following our initial delight with the slab, a number of mistakes with the original setting out progressively surfaced, and now there's a problem with the level.

Emmanuel's answer is that any tiler worth his salt would use a levelling liquid. 'My brother uses it all the time,' he says. 'If you like we can come over and get it down in half a day. Or call up a grinder.'

Gabriel says that the differential is too marked for grinding: a grinder can take off a few millimetres, but not the amount necessary to flatten the area. He will do his best, he says, but he needs to let me know that there will always be a hump in the middle of the main floor. He will of course use levelling liquid in some areas, thicker grout in others, but as this constitutes another step, all this will mean another delay…and, of course, further expense. It does help the problem somewhat, he concedes, that the travertine is half the depth of the Indonesian marble. That's something.

But in the end, it looks beautiful, so good in fact that we have them tile the entry hall, too. If the hump is there at all, it's invisible. The furniture doesn't wobble, the tracking is flush on both sides of the lounge, and any rain that blows onto the balcony, and there isn't a great deal as it faces east, drains away in the direction of the drainage hole very satisfactorily. And the best part of all? That it's done and is not something that lies ahead.

THEN MORNING COMES

In the end, it's Monday, February 6, exactly three years from the day we moved into our 'nine-month' rental, that we take possession of our new house. This is – officially, finally, unbelievably – the advent of the evasive lock-up. The exterior doors are lockable, all doors internal and external glazed, the electrics and plumbing virtually complete.

It's late when the movers finish. They're exhausted and so are we. We all started twelve hours earlier and it's been a long day. We hand over a cheque and the trucks move off down the drive. It's ours at last.

As we perch on packing cases on the balcony and the sun begins to lose its grip on the day, a stillness settles over the site and I'm reminded of one of my favourites lines from Thomas Gray "*...and leaves the world to darkness and to me*".

I know I should feel thrilled that at last we're here, but the particular type of delight that buzzes a little at the edges is missing and won't be called forth, try as I might.

How different this is from our first evening in Lockhart Street when we'd stood in the centre of the empty family room feeling the undercurrent of freeway traffic vibrating up through the floor, hugging each other hard as we looked out over a river afire with the setting sun. How different, too, from a brief voyeuristic moment years back when I'd passed by the home of new neighbours toasting each other at the open window of their house.

At the moment, I can't say I feel anything other than exhausted, and Richard looks somewhat worse. We're not deflated exactly – not yet – but it's certainly something of an anticlimax.

I take stock of where we are right now. Although the main room, the kitchen area, the balcony, our bedroom wing, the wet areas and the downstairs flat are now tiled, over half the house is still concrete screed. The ceilings and most of the cornices are painted and we've been working our way steadily through the rooms, but we still have a long way to go. The plumbing is largely complete – complete enough to satisfy Emmanuel – but the vanities are covered with plywood templates awaiting the fitting of the marble surfaces. The kitchen is just an empty space where, someday, we'll do fun things like cooking for dinner parties, but I suspect that day is some way off. In the meantime, Richard has completed the countertop and installed a large sink in the laundry, which will double as our temporary scullery and pantry. So far, the 'paint room' with its collection of towers of dribbly tins of paint and sealer, tired-looking rollers, brushes in water, brushes in turps and paint trays has occupied an area that will be my dressing room. But since the lack of fly-wire over the window means the mosquitoes are making merry with the moisture, it makes sense we move the paint across the courtyard to one of the two empty bedrooms in what will be the guest wing.

Where we have tiled floors, we have the furniture roughly in place. So we have a bed to sleep in, a couple of armchairs and somewhere to eat, but the rest – including some sixty cartons of household objects, literally thousands of books, papers, computers, linen, plastic garbage bags full of clothes – is stacked to the ceiling in the unpainted gallery. Somewhere in all the mess, there's the only mirror in the house, but I'm not sure exactly where, and it's indicative of how low I'm feeling that I wonder why it's important.

Since we aren't too high emotionally, we don't have too far to fall which is just as well because our first night is just short of miserable. It's unbearably hot and stuffy: a 28-degree-centigrade February night. The lack of mosquito netting means that if we have the windows open, we get the mozzies too. Somehow there's no air and yet a howling gale. We don't yet have window latches on the upstairs windows, but they're wedged shut. At least, that's the way they start off. One by one, through the night, they work free. We fix them shut again, and then, just as we drop into a sweaty doze, they fly open in a gust of wind to bang in turn, one after another like a series of gunshots.

In the morning, everything inside is gritty. Sand and concrete dust. What a combination. Outside, the courtyard – that 49-square-metre sacred, spiritual space I was so keen to include in this build – is a miniature replica of the Kalahari. The two Chihuahuas are sitting on their tails in the centre of a series of lumpy dunes, big ears half-mast, looking very glum at this change of scene from their comfortable townhouse. I get the impression the new surroundings are being compared somewhat unfavourably with their early pound experiences. My sense of humour is suffering from more than lack of sleep, but it does emerge long enough for me to imagine the dogs making two calls, one of complaint to the RSPCA, the other to Paris Hilton politely requesting accommodation. Would that I could do the same.

It wasn't the darkest night of my life, Dad, but the aftermath sure falls short of a bright dawn.

Two nights later, possibly as a result of a glass or so of red, we get a rush of blood and rush around the courtyard like hoons tearing myriads of glazing stickers off the panes of glass before they have time to set hard under the ruthless sun.

Everything passes. The laundry makes a very satisfactory scullery and we set up our old barbecue in the courtyard. We adapt to its idiosyncrasies – one being its lack of sufficient heat – by putting the potatoes on to boil an hour before we need to eat. For the most part, we eat simply – steak or chops and steamed vegetables – but in time I get more adventurous and try out other staples like spaghetti bolognese. I learn that if I fry the onions, garlic and mince on the hotplate and then transfer it to a saucepan where I have my tinned tomatoes, seasoning and herbs already bubbling, I can make a reasonable sauce. The pasta itself is somewhat of a challenge, but by breaking the strands into smaller pieces and feeding it gradually into the reluctantly simmering water, it works. Since the kitchen cupboards still need to be installed, almost everything remains packed. But the lack of pots and pans and general cooking paraphernalia is a big bonus when it comes to doing the dishes. Not for the first time, I am driven to wonder at all the creative ways we complicate our lives.

There's still plenty to finish off. During the daytime, the tradies come and go. Sometimes. They still have the tendency to abandon their tools and continue to be troubled by an extraordinary assortment of family traumas, which precludes their working, but at least we're living in the house and don't have to travel to the site to meet someone who doesn't turn up.

For our part, with some difficulty, given they're two metres high and two metres wide and somewhat unwieldy to move into place, we have assembled and installed the Ikea flatpack dressing room cupboards. Having been deprived of cupboards for some months – dressing for my lecturing commitments from one of the plastic bags in the gallery in front of the mirror finally found wedged between two packing cases – it's amazing how liberating it is to step into clothes I can tweak off a hanger.

I'm slowly winning with the painting and the children are wonderful, all of them steadily supportive and encouraging with the painters among them helping out as their own lives permit. Richard's son Murray and daughter Mhairi lend a hand to paint the walls and Mhairi does a fantastic job on the intimidating lengths of cornice I've been dreading in the huge main room. My son Viv risks his life on the scaffolding to put an extra coat of Supernatural on the external windows and hangs out from the balcony with a nail gun to pin a length of wooden trim across the façade of the house. He helps Richard assemble the flatpack kitchen cupboards (again Ikea – yes, I gave way on my objection to the holey sides and they serve us very well) and paints another huge chunk of the boundary wall. Shortly after we'd purchased the land, Richard's youngest son Mal had helped his father to cut down and dig out the huge stands of lantana bush multiplying over the block, and now in this final stage Mal and his lovely wife Marceena give a final sanding to the timber doors. Tammy in Melbourne keeps my spirits afloat with her many phone calls and daily emails.

Richard works on steadily: making the plinths for the cabinets, plywood templates for what will one day be marble or granite countertops, putting up shelves in the kitchen pantry and then the party room cupboard off the laundry which will house the linen for the time being. Nothing stops him. He goes to work in the mornings, comes home to work in the evenings.

But the money continues to trickle out a lot faster than we'd planned. I lie awake. Curse the menopause that stole up on me during our time at Monash Avenue. Get hot. Get cold. Get cross too easily when I should be turning as mellow as a ripening pawpaw. Toss and turn through the nights, much like the first night here. What happens if we don't finish this house? There's so much still to do. And we're getting tired. I'd hate for this to be one of those incomplete projects, something we're always going to finish, but never quite manage. I'd hate it because it would be a project I failed. But I fear it, too, for the debt it'll leave in its wake. If something happens to Richard, or to me, what then? This house needs us both. Where will the funds come from if we need to call in outside tradesmen? That is, if we can find any.

Whenever we bump into friends, their first question is, 'Have you finished the house yet?'

The light is already colouring the day when I give up pretending to sleep one early morning. I knot my sarong tight around me, avert my eyes from the sandy courtyard and pad through to the main room. We've started leaving the bifolds open night and day and the lack of any sort of barrier between me and the sight in front of me stops my breath. I step forward softly.

Framed by the arches, the eastern sky is a softly moving swirl of peach and apricot. The river pink and still as a salt lake. A lone kayaker glides slowly across the water, a dark shape with a paddle that revolves through air and water like the rhythmic wheel of a paddle steamer. Big drops of water softly splinter this sight of the new day. Even as I fumble for my camera, I know this moment is too large for any photograph. That while I might capture the contrast of light and dark, the outline of the boat against the orange-pink of the sky and water, the only place I can store the immense clarity contained in that moment is in some other space. It's as if I'm reborn with eyes brand new. Perfectly focused. As if everything I've ever been or done is contained in this current moment. And the next. A sense of continuation. A knowledge that in front of me is something that all the money in the world can't buy, that all the worrying from this morning to the next will never change a thing. That this scene will always be there. The colour printed on the grey and white of the early morning. The anonymity of the paddler. The edges of silence, both empty and full. A message that I just have to be. That to do simply nothing is to appreciate this house. That it will shortly steal my heart. And that life just is the way it is. Never say never, warns the spirit of my mother.

Easter is fast approaching and with it our last chance to take advantage of the last of the warm weather to lay turf before the winter rains and spring growth. After a fair amount of research, we decide on a new variety, Sir Walter, a soft buffalo grass that comes highly recommended. As we'll be surrounded by a fair amount of concrete – three of the neighbouring properties have virtually no garden as well as our own bitumen driveway and forecourt – predominately for its cooling properties, we plan to use grass in at least two areas of the main garden.

But, upstairs, since the arcades around the perimeter of the courtyard are now complete (finally tiled by an Indonesian tiler in the diagonal pattern of cream and terracotta we had originally envisaged), it's the courtyard that gets the attention first.

THEN MORNING COMES

We spend each evening of the week before the rolls of turf are delivered preparing the site, which means digging out the rubbish and then once we've got it clear, tying a rope to each end of a heavy beam and dragging it back and forth over the sand like a pair of pack donkeys. Finally, the sand is so smooth, silky and level that the only dents are the tiny footprints of the little dogs tracking back and forth.

Richard's son Murray, over from Sydney for a few days, kindly offers to help on the day we lay it. Fortunately. These rolls are heavy. All three of us work like sous chefs in Tetsuya's kitchen on a Saturday night. As Murray runs up the stairs with roll after roll, we attempt to keep up with him. Richard sets each in place and gives it a flick so it becomes a runner of green while I, being a Virgo and thus the pedantic one, twitch and tug so it just nudges its neighbour and water it in well while the next is being laid. Towards the end of the day, we find to our delight we've miscalculated and we have enough rolls left to do the drying green in the back garden.

We're too exhausted to appreciate it properly that night, but the following morning we wake to look out onto a magic blanket of green, cool and already luscious-looking grass. Somehow it's the first step to the house fulfilling its own dream. Although I don't know it at this moment, the sight of that huge green square of turf after the hot sand and rubble of these many months sets up a smile inside me destined to repeat itself a multiple of times each day for as long as I live here.

AN END IN SIGHT

Once winter comes, work on what will one day be the garden has to take place alongside our efforts inside the house, and we need to get a move on. But first up, we need to complete the infrastructure by finalising the retaining walls, putting in the limestone steps up the side of the block and laying the red bitumen driveway. The water in the old bore has to be tested for salinity, recommissioned, and the reticulation piping laid in time for spring planting.

During our years of frustration in the rental, we had purchased eight small olive trees we'd planted up in pots. Once the limestone wall was up between ourselves and the house in front, these plants – carefully protected from the worst of the builders' rubble and in constant danger from the heavy gates hefted from place to place – were the first to go in. A year later, they're already above the once-contentious wall, obscuring the neighbours' washing line and well on the way to giving both houses total privacy. Another early purchase we had potted up to plant on moving in were three pomegranate trees that in time will shade and soften the big north wall of the house.

Aside from that we have a *tabula rasa* in terms of an area that still resembles a building site. We have plenty of ideas, but nothing cohesive, no overall plan aside from two strong determinations: firstly, that the garden and everything in it will be grown as far as possible without chemicals and, secondly, that everything we plant will be productive or useful in some way whether it be in terms of shade, food, flora, perfume or general ecology.

A landscaping course that optimistically we had done far too early (along with the kitchen design course, the owner-builder course and the colour-coordination course), comes in handy in terms of preparing the soil and generating the idea of creating the garden in zones, just as we have done with the house. The driveway, forecourt and front garden form the first of these, the side garden the next and the back garden the third. The courtyard is a zone of its own.

In terms of soil improvement and reticulation, these zones need to be tackled concurrently and clearly and, given the appallingly sandy soil in Perth, the first step is to do something to turn sand into soil. We've both inherited 'gardens' in the past where the soil – be it sand or clay – had not been improved, and to try to grow anything in those circumstances is more often than not frustratingly unsuccessful. So we decide on a two-pronged assault on our pad of sand. Once we've cleared and levelled the site as best we can, Richard sprinkles and digs in bentonite clay to improve the nutrient and water-holding capacity. Secondly, the olive and pomegranate trees are doing so well it's clear that the 'vege-mix' we've used contains everything needed to keep plants happy, and we get enough delivered to spread thickly over the entire garden area.

Tammy and her husband Alex give us a worm farm as a moving-in present and before long we have buckets of worm juice we dilute 1:10 and which we credit for the almost 'instant' garden we get that first summer. But there's another rather unexpected bonus to this, too, one caused strangely enough by neglect. Over this first winter, we're so busy with soil and reticulation that attention to the worm garden begins and ends with dropping our food scraps into the top section and extracting the juice from below. When the castings built up to the point where we could no longer shut the lid, I had dumped them into one of the planters at the back of the block designated for eventual use as the vegetable garden. Two or three months later, when I have reason to climb the steps to that planter, I'm greeted by a jungle of vigorous vegetable plants. Dozens of tomatoes, paprika and eggplant are setting fruit and pumpkin vines are already starting to snake down the steps. Together, the castings and the winter rains have provided us with a vegetable garden free for the harvesting. By the middle of summer, we have so many cherry tomatoes that I dry tray after tray and preserve them in oil, which sees us well into the next winter season. And our chilled paprika soup with fried garlicky croutons is a huge hit at one of our early dinner parties.

Lining the edge of the driveway is easy. For a long time we've had our heart set on a hedge of *mutabilis chinensis*, the tough and beautiful Old China roses that flower all year round and never need deadheading. In fact, we find that, aside from reticulation and a little fertilizer from time to time, the only upkeep is running the clippers across the top and along the sides of the hedge three or four times a year. The mix of light apricot, pink and cerise blooms covering the bushes is both profuse and delicate; looking down from the house it's as if a kaleidoscope of butterflies lines the route.

We have no trouble planning the side garden either. Once the steep flight of limestone steps is in place, we kid ourselves it resembles the Spanish Steps in Rome and this area quickly becomes the Spanish garden. One of my books has photographs of the gardens in Spain's Alhambra Palace and I return again and again to one of my photos of its archway of coloured roses. This can be duplicated here. Richard works out the dimensions for hoops of galvanized steel piping. We set up the arches over the Easter break and by the following summer a cascade of red, yellow and pink roses spills out over the stretch of lush grass to shade the walkway to the steps.

But the front garden is more difficult. There's not a lot of it in terms of actual space – only about 60 square metres – and it has to be all things to the two of us. Already we have our row of screening olive trees along the front border. Richard wants at least some lawn to offset the rather austere effect of the bitumen forecourt. I think a water feature of some description would be attractive, although neither of us has been impressed so far by the many water walls and Balinese-type fountains we've investigated. We jointly lust after tropical fruit trees that we know will do well in the warm, moist, micro-culture created by the combination of a small space containing water surrounded by tall walls and buildings. Optimistically we can already taste mangoes, avocados and even paw paws. Lastly, it has to complement the character of the house. All this in one small space. We're lost. We need help.

I call around and receive some outrageous quotes before a friend puts me in touch with Linda of Living Designs who comes to see the project two days later.

'There are a dozen ways you can tackle this,' she says as we walk the space. She stops, squints into the sky and then looks back up at the house. 'The area's going to be viewed from two predominant angles, isn't it? From above looking down from the balcony, and then from the forecourt as you drive or walk in. From above, a *parterre* garden would look gorgeous – that's the space divided up into small areas each containing a collection of different plants or shrubs – with perhaps a round pond with a fountain in the middle to give you the water feature you'd like.

'Or you might build up a bank on either side and have a small stream that wends its way through the area…

'Or…' she rubs her chin, thinking, looks back at the house again. 'Your house has a sort of Hispanic-Moorish character doesn't it? A rill would work well.'

'A rill?'

'Yes, a narrow channel that leads from an overflowing bowl into a pond. They're common in Spain and other parts of the Mediterranean. Since you've already got your olive trees in place that would blend perfectly. And, then, let me see. The tropical fruit is going to do best against that enormous boundary wall and will eventually provide quite a pleasant backdrop as well. You might put in a border of small limestone blocks to delineate the area between the lawn and a garden bed at the base of the olive trees. I'll give it some thought and come up with some drawings for you.'

And for a very reasonable fee and in a short space of time, she drops around three very different garden designs. All attractive, but for us the one that works best is a longish rectangular pond with water lilies and bubble jets surrounded by a grassed area, again reminiscent of the Alhambra although, of course, on a micro-scale. At last, we've stumbled across someone who understands what we are trying to create in terms of atmosphere.

We follow Linda's brief. Dave comes back to delineate the space with more limestone blocks and then we get in a small bobcat to scoop out the sand for the pond.

A young man – who's on a justifiable high because he's just sold his first novel to Random House on the basis of two chapters in a submission query – gives us some advice which turns out to be spot on.

'Probably the most important thing with a pond is to get the balance right which'll take a little while to do. Once it all starts flowing, you'll find the fish thrive, the algae will reduce and the water lilies'll jump away. But that's not going to happen right away. Oh yes, and your lilies are going to lose their leaves in winter and it'll look as though nothing's happening, but it is… Although you can't see it, that's their real growth time when they're putting on more root. With eight metres of pond, four plants is plenty.'

We buy the fish from him, too: ten small goldfish, one of which starts growing from the moment it swims free of its plastic bag until it's the size of a small koi. President Hoover, Richard christens this fish, as we watch him beat the others out of the way as he cruises with a permanently open mouth to suck up the fragments of fish food. A big fish in a small pond the President may be, but he's clearly leader of this school that soon doubles in size and varies from black to gold and from striped to spotted. We take to sitting on the low limestone wall with our cups of tea and coffee during gardening breaks. It's a Sunday sport to watch the President bully his team and the effect on our blood pressure is probably about the same as watching fish in an aquarium. Although I suspect it's got a long way to go before it returns to pre-build level.

But everyone's blood pressure takes a hike a few days later. The downstairs flat is now complete and Tammy has been staying there during her business trips to and from Melbourne. One morning she comes up for breakfast wrinkling her nose.

'There's a not-very-nice smell in the bathroom downstairs.'

'What sort of not nice?'

'Well, you know, not nice at all. Like bad. Smell it for yourself.'

She's right. It's not only not nice, but a downright disgusting, unflushed, stinky-toilet smell.

When Emmanuel sends the plumber to investigate, it appears the problem lies upstairs in Richard's toilet.

'Toilet's clogged,' states the plumber's mate, a man who's so laid back, he has trouble standing upright.

'Already? We've only been in a few months. And I can't say I've had a clogged toilet in years, perhaps ever.'

'Well, this one's jammed up.' I can't say his look is exactly accusing, but it's pointed enough to move me to add that this is Richard's toilet anyway. 'I'll have to find exactly where the problem lies,' he says. 'Always difficult these things.'

From the difficulties we've had getting the plumber to rectify his many mistakes and oversights, I imagine that even getting out of bed would pose a problem.

But to fix things, he needs me, too, so I spend the better part of the next two hours flushing the toilet while he works on unclogging it from below until he pronounces himself satisfied the problem is sorted.

'Runs beautifully now.'

'So what was the problem, do you think?'

Eyes me again. 'Clogged.' And we have to leave it there as he lumbers off down the driveway.

But a week or so later, as I attach a hose to a tap on the wall outside the flat, I notice the smell again. Worse than ever.

This time Emmanuel turns up himself. He believes the problem is inside the flat itself, so we inspect the bathroom.

'Ah!' He spies the smart chrome waste pipe waiting to be attached to a downstairs washing machine we haven't yet had the time or money to purchase. 'There you are. That's your problem, there.' He goes over to the waste, bends down, sniffs and stands up nodding. 'Yes, I thought as much. The smell is coming up through that pipe there. When are you going to link it up?'

'We're not. Well, not for some time yet. It's just there in case we ever need the flat to be totally self-contained.'

'Well, you'll have to do something about it. Even if you put a plastic bag over the pipe for the moment. Secure it with an elastic band…'

Which we do, wait a few more days, but the smell doesn't go away. We call him again, but he's unconvinced there's a problem. We know there is. We mention that it's severe enough to constitute a health issue.

Two days later there's a shout from Richard.

'For heaven's sake! Just look at this!' He's scraped the earth away from the house foundations outside the flat and he's leaning on his garden spade watching as a thick brown sludge oozes out of a crack in the wall. 'That's why it smells. Sewerage. In the walls of the house itself!'

This time the plumber returns so fast, it's clear he's found another gear.

'Cracked pipe,' he pronounces. He sticks his thumbs through his belt loops as emphasis he's suspected this all along.

'In the wall? How?' After two other guesses have turned out to be wrong, I'm skeptical, but certainly something's cracked.

'Brick, probably,' he says. 'That's what they do. Must've been dropped down the pipe before the toilet was connected.'

Just who *they* are, we don't know, but in order to fix the problem a fairly large hole of about a metre in diameter is bashed in the outer wall. The section of pipe is replaced, but we sit with the hole for weeks until Rolf has time to come back to re-brick it. And then it's back into our painty gear to reseal and repaint.

Insulation is something that's been on our minds for some time. Within the confines of the block orientation, which runs roughly east-west, and our obvious desire to maximise river views, we've built as solar-sensitive a house as is economical practical.

Meanwhile we learn to live in this house, adapt to its ways. In the hot Perth summer, the deep balcony keeps the eastern sun off the stretch of bifolds along the front, so there are only blinds to adjust for a few hours in the study and breakfast room. We had decided against windows in the vulnerable west-facing wall of the gallery which not only makes it cooler but also enables an uninterrupted stretch of wall for our art collection. The roofed arcade along our bedroom wing protects these rooms from the sun that beats into the courtyard and the louvre windows either side of our bedhead allow breezes to filter through the room all year round. In the main room, we leave the two sets of bifolds open day and night for most of the time from November through April, spending part of our days and evenings virtually outdoors. Despite our proximity to the river, mosquitoes are rarely a problem in summer and flies only a nuisance when there's a hot wind from the east. In winter, the sun flows into the breakfast room and in the study I write in a sunbeam for the first two or three hours of each day. This time of year we switch our lunchtime break from the front balcony (which becomes distinctly chilly) to the sunny courtyard. We install fans: two in the main room, one in the dining area and another in our bedroom. The next step is roof insulation, but first we have to get another manhole installed in the laundry ceiling. One is not enough in a house this size where the roof space is so tight you have to crawl from one area to another.

'I'll see if I can get someone in to do it,' I say to Richard.

'Why?'

'Because. Just because you have enough on with the library shelves at the moment. You've got too much on altogether, actually.'

He hates it, I know, that anything here is done by someone else (apart from Tangea), but in a few cases, it makes sense. There's simply not enough time to do everything.

The day the tradesman comes is so wet and blustery I thank the gods it's not an outside job; the memories of any excuse at all for the trades not to turn up during the build are still tender.

He's finished in no time as it turns out and he's back in the study wanting his cheque.

'All set. But you'll never guess what I've just seen.'

'No. What?'

'Well, that was the darndest thing,' he says in a North American accent. Shakes his head. 'Never seen anything like it before. You see out there?' He nods in the direction of the courtyard, silvery right now with the sheeting rain. 'Well, I was walking back along that outside corridor you have there, when there was a soft boom sound, like, and the rain, the rain just lifted up and completely disappeared for a few seconds. For long enough for me to stop and stand and wonder whether it were going to come back down again. In the end, it did. Weird it was. Bit of a mystery.'

He leaves, still shaking his head.

So insulation is next, but just what insulation to choose of the many products on the market? Since we have downlights through the house, we don't like the idea of fibreglass batts given the possibility of fibres leaching through the gaps. Richard has had the blow-in wood fibre in the past with success, but I'm dubious about this for a similar reason. We investigate wool, expensive but tempting. And then Richard finds a new green alternative: aircell sheeting. We call around, but currently it's only available for commercial installations and not viable, I'm told, for the comparatively small quantity we need.

'Why not?' This is my sixth phone call and I've progressed from my initial discussions with the original company in the Eastern States to finding someone locally who actually installs it here.

'It's just not worth our while.' His voice is getting that thin edge which means, Look, I'm a busy man, lady. I want to get on with my day and making a living.

'But Bunnings sells it. That must mean someone can install it.' A thought occurs to me. 'I can try asking them for a contact, but I thought…'

He sighs. 'Hang on a sec. There *is* someone. Old chap, but probably still the best in the business. Knows ceiling installation inside out. Don't know whether he's still doing it, but his name's Harry and this phone number might still work. Other than that, I can't help you.' He repeats the phone number and hangs up on my thanks.

He's right, Harry isn't young, but he looks fitter and wirier than most men half his age. He turns up to view the job with his offsider, a tall dark-looking fellow who says nothing, but stands in the main room with his arms folded and a frown on his face as he glares across at the river.

Harry, on the other hand, has a lot to say. But beyond asking whether we have a ladder available so he won't have to bring his own up the stairs, checking that we have a manhole and taking the dimensions from a copy of the plan, nothing he says has any relevance at all to ceiling installation.

In fact, I can't remember what we talked about so animatedly and I have absolutely no idea how we got on to the topic of women being chopped up, blended and quick-frozen. We'd arrived at the top of the stairs ready to descend when he stopped to elucidate and for the next minutes – or was it hours? – his monologue was relentless. I listened in horror, caught in the glare of an invisible spotlight and unable to move until I gathered my wits enough to gallop down the stairs in the middle of the flow.

Just what was it that freaked me out? The ghoulish topic itself or the ease with which he brought it up? Or my inability to move, as if I were quick-frozen myself.

I'm still shaking when I call Toni.

'Help. There's no way, absolutely no way, we can go ahead with him. I can't be here by myself while he does this job. He's…frightening.'

'What sort of frightening. Big and intimidating?'

'No, not really. Opposite. Small and wiry. And not particularly young.' I remember the sour-looking apprentice who Harry had volunteered was from Jamaica. 'But his helper is huge.'

'Can't Richard be there?'

'For the two or three days it's going to take? No. But the alternative is we can't have the insulation we'd like. I wonder whether I'm being totally, ridiculously, stupid.'

I do wonder, but on the other hand in the past when I've had this sort of chilled reaction to a person or place, there's always been a reason.

'I could call you,' Toni says. 'I could call you a few times and perhaps Richard could, too.'

Richard and I debate and finally we decide to go ahead.

The fact that I have a manuscript to finish off and the usual deadline that goes with it means there's no difficulty being busy when they arrive. I'm organized for the visit this end. The ladder is in place and the manhole open when they climb the stairs with the rolls of insulation. I only half-turn from my feverish typing, keep my greeting short, but if Harry notices my terseness, it doesn't deter him. The big man goes down for another load while he stops to talk.

I explain about the deadline I have to meet. And then, to take the edge off my brisk manner, since he's still standing beside me as I turn back to my computer, I ask politely if there's anything he needs.

'I need somewhere I can cut up the sheets,' he says. 'Somewhere I can spread the stuff out to cut up with scissors. And a hard surface where I can use this.'

I look up. He's here in my sunny study, standing half a metre away from me with a knife in his hand. It may simply have been a Stanley blade, I don't know, because I think I'd rather not know. But even a Stanley can do some damage. It's broad daylight with the birds singing out there, and this place is full of sun and light, not Hitchcock dark and silent with music building in the background. That's what I tell myself. Along with, be cool. Imagination is a two-edged sword.

I think he'd rather do his work on the floor behind my back in the study, but there's no way I'm letting him stop in here. So I suggest, rather firmly, that he take advantage of the beautiful weather and use the balcony. That way I can keep an eye on him through the window to my right and before long he's settled himself quite comfortably cross-legged on the floor. Looks almost meditative as he crafts the neat collars that will be placed around the downlights.

I'm starting to relax, to insert myself back into the story I'm crafting, when I hear a curse, not quite loud, not quite muffled. Behind me, some twelve metres away, on the other side of the main room, the big man is two or three steps up the ladder, his head and shoulders in the roof space, talking to himself. I glance sideways through the study window to where Harry sits chopping up insulation and taking no notice at all.

The monologue gets louder and louder. The words separate to become recognizable as a steady flow of invective. Most of the words I'm well acquainted with, some quite new. But I've never heard so many swear words joined together in an unending string in quite this way. Harry doesn't even look up. He still looks as if he's meditating. And he's quite unmoved by the escalating tirade, totally unperturbed, as if this is a regular event. But it's clear his assistant is extremely unhappy about something and the words quickly become loud enough to fill in the picture. Tucked into the rant emerges the odd phrase about rich people who live on the river, total thoughtlessness, impossibly cramped roof space. Harry may be untroubled, but it's hard to work alongside this unhappy outpouring which continues for what is an extraordinary length of time for such a restricted glossary of words. When, eventually, the man hefts himself upwards, the outburst turns to muttering and then vanishes entirely until the only noise in the house is the clicking of computer keys.

I jump a mile high when Harry speaks behind me. 'Sorry about the raving. He does that sometimes.'

I spin my chair around. No knife. 'He sounds upset. Very upset about something…'

'Yes, he gets like that from time to time. Means no harm. He's all right now and he's excellent at what he does.'

Harry and his assistant complete the job in two days. They do a great job and we're delighted with the insulation which cools the house ten degrees or more. This is one time when my sixth sense is fortunately off the mark. He compliments us on the garden as he leaves, offers to lend me his book on roses. I thank him, but tell him that I have lots of my own rose books and, besides, I prefer not to borrow books. Which is true.

Gradually the "to do" list becomes more manageable as we settle down to the business of living and working in this house that each day becomes more of a home.

A pair of welcome swallows have built their nest on top of a power point three metres above the ground in the garage. Each spring they have chicks and the whole family swoops in figures of eight around and about our heads when we're out walking the little dogs in the park.

A Chinese friend comes to visit, sees the nest. 'They're lucky, those birds. Bring luck. People in Hong Kong or China would pay a lot of money for a nest like that.'

We rig up a perch for them along one wall of the garage and they stay with us for several years making very little mess and providing endless delight as they dive in and out. And remind me of the swallows in the rafters of the chapel on Rottnest Island.

WHAT'S IN A NAME?

It's the naming of this property we tackle next. I think back to the houses we've owned and the unimaginative labels we've stuck on them even as our minds might conjure up quite another picture. Over the last few years, there's been Corkhill Street, Kintail Road, Lockhart Street and Monash Avenue: street tags, frosty and impersonal, that act like surnames to smother the real fact of the matter that these are homes that have played a part in the drift and drafting of our lives.

For ages, we'd searched for an appropriate title for Lockhart Street, but the names we came up with were either too cutesy or too grand, failing totally to express what it was that house meant to us. My mother's last house after many moves around East Africa comes to mind.

Mum had been extraordinarily proud of that house in Nairobi, Kenya. It was the first, I think, they'd built together and for some reason she chose a Black Forest design with a steeply pitched roof, tiled in black, with dormer windows front and back. Inside she had pale Loliondo wood floors throughout – the beautiful lightly-streaked wood otherwise known as Ironwood that comes from the trees of the olive family – and wrought iron gates to seal off the bedroom wing at night. She was interviewed by one of the glossy home magazines about the building of the house, and on the cover of that issue she stares proudly into the sun with the house and its avenue of Jacaranda trees behind her.

Her sixteen years in Africa had begun just after World War II when she travelled out to Southern Rhodesia on a converted warship to join the man who was to become my father. That last house my parents had in Nairobi represented both a peak and a conclusion to a period of dreams come true for the young English woman who had trained to be a tailor and who had left her brothers and sisters back home in Middlesex tut-tutting about her wild ways. 'June's like a rambling rose,' my Aunt Ruby had cautioned Dad before he married her. 'Don't think you'll ever tame her.' And I don't think my father ever tried. Instead he gave her what she wanted: adventure. My parents were married for nearly thirty years and during that time, they lived in a series of mainly rented homes throughout central, southern and eastern Africa and, later, in the south and west of Australia, their many homes together ending with the house they built themselves brick-by-brick in the Perth hills when they were no longer young. She had guts, my Mum.

And so it was that many years after I'd left as a teenager I returned to Nairobi on a sort of pilgrimage to visit this house she'd loved so much and which had once been the toast of the town.

Somewhat to my surprise, at first sight nothing much had changed. I had feared that the fields in front of the house – which from time to time were inhabited by a small herd of elephant – would be built up by now, a sea of roofs with the black pitch sticking awkwardly out of the middle. Or that the avenue of purple Jacaranda trees that had been planted by the Catholic nuns to link their convent to the monastery on the other side of town would have been ripped out in the name of development. But, no, the trees were still there and the house looked the same, only the cedar cladding on the top half needed a coat of linseed oil. The only obvious change was in the garden, now barren, with the roses, hibiscus and poinsettia trees long gone, and the dirt cracked and curling like a layer of chocolate that has melted and re-set, as clay soils tend to do in that part of the world. And when I looked more closely, I saw that each tree in the avenue had a chain attached, the other end locked around a bicycle wheel.

The driver kept the engine running. I tapped him lightly on the shoulder.

'I don't understand? All those bikes?'

'Hostel. Now a hostel for students, Memsahib. Many, very many, people live here.'

I went to get out, put my hand on the door handle. My husband put his hand on my shoulder.

'Don't.' he said, his voice gentle. 'Leave it. Preserve it as it was.'

But I couldn't. I heard the engine revving behind me as I walked towards the open front door. Stood outside, looking in. Inside it was filled with beds. Or futons, really, covering the wood floor. Many, as the driver had said.

Back in the car, even if I could have said something, there was really nothing to say. Suddenly I was fiercely glad my mother was dead. She hadn't wanted to leave that house and now that dream – that house as it once was – was locked up with her. My sadness – no longer hers – was that she had always wanted to name it and never did.

Her story returns to me because with this house, too, we've procrastinated. But now my son Viv's wedding to his gorgeous Clare is imminent. Our home is about to host 110 guests for the reception. And this turns out to be the event that starts us brainstorming names in earnest.

What can we call a house that, jointly, we've brought into being? A name that will incorporate the good energy that's been part of this house and that has, despite the various difficulties of the project, asserted itself time and again since its inception? Where can we find a name that will suit the house itself without being pretentious, that won't impose on the building its own stamp of arrogance or expectation?

Over the past couple of years, we've dreamed up and discarded dozens of names and I'm increasingly frustrated and more than a little despondent it'll end up nameless like all the rest. Because I know that if you don't name a place when it's young, it's a bit like delaying a renovation you finally get around to only when you sell and I'm determined that won't happen.

In the end, it comes to pass quite naturally. Of all the names we've come up with and discarded, I still liked *Chikupi*, the name of the old Zambian homestead that Ethnée Holmes à Court had talked about so often when we were working on her book. Richard is not so keen.

'Why do you like it so much?'

'Because it has a good ring. Because, oh I don't know, because the *chi* part of it says breath, energy… the good energy…the vital *chi*…'

'What's "good" in Swahili, then? *M'zuri*? How about calling it *M'zuri*?'

'Yes. Excellent. That's good. Or maybe even better, how about this? How about combining the two: the energy and the good, the *chi* and the *zuri*? How about calling it *ChiZuri*…the good energy?' As with everything else we've tackled together, our brainstorming combines our thoughts to produce a spiral of inspiration which produces the result we're after.

A woman who specializes in enamel house nameplates slips our sign into her busy agenda and a week later, the day before the wedding, we fix it to the pillar at the bottom of the driveway. We're too busy with the wedding preparations to give it the ceremony it deserves but, officially, *ChiZuri* has come to be.

ChiZuri stands proud this hot November day with the temperature a sticky 37 degrees centigrade. My soon-to-be daughter-in-law Clare wants huge vases of flowers and so we borrow tall glass containers a metre high and my stepsister-friend Michele has her usual wonderful way with them. She has decided to do up a number of luscious combinations of white Asian lilies, tall-stemmed white roses and white lizzianthus, the borrowed vases positioned in the hallway just inside the front door and again rearing up either side of the stairs on the top floor.

The children's Aunty Pat, now in her mid-eighties and over from England for her nephew's wedding, vies with Michele for the right to do the flowers. She fixes Michele with a steady gaze from her dark brown eyes. 'I do them for the Church, you know,' she says. 'Back in Stevenage. Every week.' But Michele is equally keen to arrange these flowers. She cuts the furry pollen-coated anthers out of the lilies, trims stems, fills the vases with water crystals. While Pat hovers. In the end, I suggest that Pat do the arrangement for the powder room. And then they're both happy. Between them they fill the pottery urns on the balcony with trailing white petunias, make themselves a pot of tea. And talk.

Every couple of metres up the length of the driveway, on the tops of the limestone walls and in the borders of the flower beds, we set the little oil lamps they use for religious ceremonies and festive occasions in Bali. Small tongues of flame on short poles designed to flicker above the hedge and about the garden. There are sixty of them in all, these fragile, dubiously fired clay lamps. Last trip to Ubud became a search for these *lampu*, available at a particular stall in the markets, and Toni and her Rog bravely brought a batch home for us on their recent visit to Bali.

Three hours later, Michele gets a call from her husband.

'Where are you for Christ's sake?'

'Just coming,' she yells into the phone, dragging her equipment to her car. She jumps in. Sticks her head out the window of the big four wheel drive.

'Tangea. Give in, why don't you? Put on the air conditioning? The flowers. They should be all right until tomorrow, but phewf, it's hot. Really hot. They need cool.'

The following day when we arrive back from the ceremony, it's hotter still. I put out a call for all hands to put the final touches to the decorations. Pat shunts both her age and the heat to one side, working like mad to fill split lengths of white-painted bamboo with sprays of iceberg roses which she places on the window sills along the arcades. Later that night she dances me into exhausted admiration of her exuberant energy.

For tonight, there's a wooden dance floor set up in the centre of the courtyard and tall bar tables set around the perimeter beside each of the pillars. Acting on another idea we've cadged from our trips to Bali, Richard has rigged up some cabling under the guttering and ten round paper lanterns jut out like frosty moons over the tables.

Clare's parents have financed everything: the champagne, the wines and the expensively catered meal. The succulent dishes are served from the long table in the gallery which is backed by a mass of fifty lights – white candles of varied shapes and sizes – that glow like a wall of flame. The disc jockey fires up. And the show is on.

Moving between the guests, I hear snatches of conversation.

'*ChiZuri*. Strange name. Why on earth did they call the house that?'

And Paul, the children's cousin, trying gravely to answer, gets about as close as we could ourselves.

'It's Swahili, the language of East Africa. That's part of it. Because they both come from there. Or spent time there. It means good. A good spirit associated with the house.'

And one couple to another couple. Perfectly serious. 'Why haven't we heard of this reception venue before?'

There's so much going on I think I'm the only one to see it, but the full moon tonight plays its special part. Anchored in the night sky directly opposite the house, it casts a ribbon of speckled mica across the river from shore to share, the rippling beam rich with promise.

So much for the optimistic message on our Christmas card in 2005. Lock-up is delayed and it will now be February before the much anticipated moving day.

As most of you know, at long last this Christmas finds us in the middle of our move to our new home. Please note our new address at

Chizuri

11 Salter Point Parade
Salter Point Western Australia 6152
Tel/fax 9450 3206

As I walk into the lounge early, one recognizes what a sunset

The arcades tiled with the Indonesian tiles in the diamond pattern we'd hoped for.

The side garden with its arbour of climbing roses leading to the "Spanish Steps" in the background.

And now for landscaping the front garden. The retaining and setting-out of the pond area begins.

The internal courtyard finally lush and green with the gallery in the background and a canopy of fruiting grapevines for shade.

And before too long the front garden is complete with its backdrop of prolific mango and avocado trees, a pond full of happy fish and water lilies with the screening olive trees on one side and a row of standard roses on the other.

The downstairs hallway with the curved wall Rolf worked so hard to perfect.

From the top of the stairs, a view of the main room and kitchen with its travertine tiling. *Photo courtesy Greg Hocking.*

Harvest

LATER

If our build were featured in the popular television series *Grand Designs*, it's at this early point in its life cycle that Kevin McCloud would arrive at the bottom of the driveway to deliver his final pronouncement.

The camera would track him walking up the drive along the avenue of roses, his face a mask of slightly skeptical expectation, his eyes raised towards the house, his fingertips lightly touching. On reaching the forecourt he would pivot on one heel with the building at his back looming high into the endlessness of the Perth-blue sky.

Turn slowly to face the camera.

'I can't believe the difficulties this couple have had with this house,' he would say. 'A large part of their problem, of course, was that they elected to end their contract with the builder at lock-up stage…and no one knew exactly where the responsibility of each began and ended.

'It didn't make it any easier that they were both working as well as managing parts of the project – *and* doing a great deal of the hands-on work on this site themselves.

'And none of this was helped by the boom. Prices sky-rocketed, and although they were to some extent protected by a fixed-price contract, inevitably this not only squeezed the builder financially but also affected the owners who had opted to finance the completion of the building… normally about thirty per cent of the whole project, but I suspect it's a lot more in this case.

'Add to this the sheer idiocy of the times. Think of it: those skilled workers that weren't lured up to the north of the State by promises of crazy money generated by the resources boom were siphoned to growing cities like Mandurah just south of the metro area. Builders lost all but the most loyal of their teams and those that were left were under the hammer to such an extent many cracked under the pressure.

'I know they've had an extremely tight budget for this build…and I'm very interested to see what they've made of it.'

And I, in turn, wonder what he'd think of it. Because I know each tile and every corner of this house. I see the finishing touches it still lacks, a touch-up of paint here, a missing fragment of grout there. And there's still additional furniture to be built in. But does anyone else see this? I wonder.

But it may just be that Kevin's reaction wouldn't be much different to that of the vast majority of the literally hundreds of people that have attended this house in the course of its short life for dinners, charity, engagement, wedding and birthday parties.

The house itself is unusual, yes, with its river panorama framed by the pillars, with the grassed courtyard scented with frangipani, jasmine and gardenias under-planted with herbs for the kitchen, with the tiled arcades and with the three sets of bifolds that enable the complete space from the edge of the balcony to the back wall of the gallery to be opened up into one large whole. Or to be closed down into separate rooms – or zones – so the entire area doesn't have to be heated or cooled. Or regularly cleaned.

But it's something more that causes people to react the way they do, something that can't be achieved by money alone, something that creates the compliments *ChiZuri* attracts at parties and the thank-you cards that follow. An intangible something that's an integral part of this house. And whether it's the love that's been poured into it, the incense that burned holes in the balcony of its surrogate every day of its build, the Reiki blessings or the good wishes sealed into its foundations or all of the above, who can say?

But then, having made his appraisal of the building, Kevin would smilingly ask the hard question.

Settles back on the couch with a slight smile, fingertips once again touching.

'I know you had a tight budget for the building of this house, didn't you? How did it work out in the end?'

That's a difficult one to answer because (a) we're not quite 'at the end' (is one ever?) and (b) Richard and I are divided as to how much we've actually spent. So far neither of us have quite had the courage to go through the piles of receipts, bank statements and cheque stubs in an attempt to tot it up.

But while there's no question it made a total mockery of the initial budget and cost us well over double the sum of money originally available, someone was looking after us back there in Lockhart Street the day we decided to buy the investment properties. The boom meant that although our house cost considerably more than we could have guessed, the value of the other real estate was keeping pace. So, all in all, we could still afford to replace our painty gear with street clothes. With our investment properties progressively selling, we came out mortgage-free. Well, close.

Would we do it again? We're asked that a lot. I don't know. It takes very little for me to make a suggestion with regard to a possible new build, for Richard to reach for his pen and the back of an envelope, and our mutual enthusiasm to escalate. Yes, some people are certainly suckers for punishment, as my father would say. But then I think of the sleepless nights worrying about money. Or, the absolute worst – which used to keep me tossing through the nights during the *après*-lock-up period – what if something happened to either of us and the house had to be put on the market atrociously incomplete?

And yet, building has an addictive edge to it, a headiness like being in love, with its very uncertainty or potential difficulty lending it attraction. I remember standing in the temporary builder's road with Emmanuel one day, discussing another project he said he'd been asked to tender for.

'It's a difficult one,' he said. 'Several storeys with an infinity pool. Big budget.' He bit his bottom lip, turned to me. 'It would be a challenge, but I like a challenge.'

So what would Kevin McCloud state in his final wrap-up? I think I'd like him to say something like this.

Closeup.

'By their own admission, this couple bit off more than they could reasonably chew. Despite all their planning, from what they've told me, this build *evolved*. And it kept on changing and growing until it finally emerged as something quite different from the plan of the one-bedroom retirement house they started with.

'Quite apart from the physical effort, there's absolutely no question of the love and thought that's been poured into every detail of this building. As a result, they have a house which simply glows with a pride and confidence in every aspect of itself and, despite all the ups and downs, they've ended up with a splendid home inspired by the countries in which they've lived and travelled and has all the elements they need for their particular lifestyle.

'The lushness of the central courtyard – that both joins and separates the living areas – makes this house and its garden absolutely seamless, one so much part and parcel of the other. The very spirit of this fragrant, central space pervades every room…'

Swings from his view of the courtyard to face the river.

'And as for this. Imagine walking from the bedroom into this room each morning…towards this expanse of blue water framed so beautifully by these pillars. It'd be like living in a Greek villa – every day of your life.'

Leans towards camera, drops his voice to a loud whisper.

'I would say they're *very, very* lucky people.'

Fade out. Gently.

I would agree with Kevin. We are very lucky people. Lucky to have this house that's so much a home. Lucky it turned out as well as it did. That it grew into itself.

But *luck* is too ephemeral, too unreliable, a word to describe the whole of what *ChiZuri* means to us.

This house has given us a shared history, that bonding we were after in the first place that only comes about through serious stuff like conception, gestation and the bringing forth of something you've jointly created into real time. Never easy and, yes, relentless, but at the same time…

'Do you remember the day,' I'll say to Richard in a hundred years' time that'll pass quicker than our speedy new kettle can boil. 'Do you remember that time we planted the frangipani tree in the courtyard and I left the hose trickling on it only to find it had disappeared under the house twenty minutes later?

'Or the ginger plant we bought from the nursery thinking it to be edible ginger, only to find it was ornamental? How, grumpily, we heeled it into a pile of vege mix, then found we needed the soil, so it was transferred to what was one day designed to be the tropical garden alongside my bathroom? And how that tiny plant grew into a jungle of lush plants, tall as the house itself, with deep green and white leaves along which, twice a year, thick ropes of flowers lay like necklets of huge pearls?

'Or the view to the river through the louvres your side of the bed past the bright tangle of bougainvillea down the narrow stretch between the house and Julio's big wall? How, at certain times of the year, it glowed so brightly in the early morning sun it looked as if Midas himself had touched that narrow corridor with a wand?

'And the moon? Do you remember, Rich, how I thought next door's had left the outside light on overnight when I woke up early one morning to see a big white globe shining onto my pillow? It took me a while of waking time to figure out it was the moon and when I turned my head to tell you that here it was, almost daylight already with the moon forgotten to go to bed, I saw the yellow sun in an identical place outside your window? And how, for that space in time, the house balanced like a seesaw between the moon and the rising sun?

'And the many, many mornings during the long build when you held me tight to cuddle away my frustration and told me how much you loved me…

'Do you remember all those things, Richard? Because I do.'

ABOUT THE AUTHOR

Tangea Tansley is the author of four novels and several works of non- and hybrid fiction. Her ninth book *The Voices in My Head*, a novel, is scheduled for publication by Dixi Books in 2023.

Of her short stories, many have been published or anthologised and have won or been runners-up in a number of national competitions; her articles, essays and reviews have appeared in national and international magazines, journals and newspapers.

She was born in Zimbabwe, grew up in East Africa and after several decades spent living and working around the world settled in Perth, Western Australia. Her professional background lies in journalism, magazine editing and publishing, university lecturing and tutoring.

For further information, see tangeatansley.com

www.ingramcontent.com/pod-product-compliance
Lightning Source LLC
Chambersburg PA
CBHW041507010526
44118CB00006B/182